SHEFFIELD HALLAM UNIVERSITY
LEARNING CENTRE
CITY CAMPUS, POND STREET,
SHEFFIELD, S1

101 641 365

D0120128

UNIVERSITY
NTRE
OM STOCK

ONE WEEK LOAN

Behind the scenes in advertising

Jeremy Bullmore

Admap

Second edition published 1998 by Admap Publications
Farm Road, Henley-on-Thames,
Oxfordshire RG9 1EJ, United Kingdom
Telephone: +44 (0) 1491 411000
Facsimile: +44 (0) 1491 571188
E-mail: admap@ntc.co.uk

First published 1991 by NTC Publications Limited.

Copyright © Jeremy Bullmore 1998
Jeremy Bullmore has asserted his right under the Copyright, Designs
and Patent Act, 1988, to be identified as the Author of this Work.

A CIP catalogue record for this book is available from the British
Library.

ISBN 1 899314 92 X

Typeset in 12/14pt Garamond MT by Admap Publications
Printed and bound in Great Britain by
Biddles Ltd, Guildford and King's Lynn

All rights reserved.
Without limiting the rights under copyright reserved above, no
parts of this publication mya be rreproduced, stored in or
introduced into a retrieval system, or transmitted, in any form
or by any means, electronic, mechanical, photocopying, recording
or otherwise, without the prior written permission of the
copyright owner.

Contents

Handwritten annotations: "— Selling of values" (next to Competitive persuasion); "Selling values" (next to Whatever happened to the Hidden Persuaders?); "— an example of Product Placement" (next to The hair restorer that didn't)

Chapters marked with an asterisk* are new for this second edition.

Foreword to the first edition

I read this book in bed last night. *Fascinating.*

It tells the story of a sensitive man who stumbled into advertising and floated to the top – without losing his entrancing sense of humour.

Everybody who chooses advertising as a career does it for the wrong reasons. Jeremy Bullmore records what it is really like to work in an advertising agency – what happens behind the scenes. In the process he reveals his professional expertise with prodigal generosity. I learned a lot.

David Ogilvy, 1991

Preface

There's all the difference in the world between having a career and working.

A career involves ladders and titles and heavy responsibilities and an oppressive expectation that you will make some form of quantifiable progress. Working – if it happens to be work you like – is almost totally enjoyable.

My formal career ended ten years ago when I left J. Walter Thompson. Since then, I've been working rather more than half of most weeks – but never breathlessly. As a non-executive director of the Guardian Media Group and WPP Group plc, I've kept close to the aquarium I used to inhabit while avoiding a second submergence.

So the 25 new chapters which have been added to this book, all written since 1988, are much less to do with the day-to-day business of advertising and marketing than some of the earlier pieces. They are also more liberated and more lofty: liberated because I've felt less constrained; and lofty because my relative detachment from the business has prompted the occasional reckless certainty.

Thanks to the ingenuity of my editor, Mallory Holland, all the new pieces have found homes in the old structure. On the contents page, they are marked with an asterisk. Most of the shorter pieces first appeared in *Marketing*, for which I've been writing a column, more or less every month, since the middle of 1995. Six chapters have been dropped.

The first edition attracted a few dedicated fans, to all of whom I'm extremely grateful. They include: Feona McEwan, who badgered both me and NTC into doing this second, bumper edition; David Stuart, who liked the book so much that he volunteered to design the new dust-jacket; and Martin

Sorrell, who must single-handedly have accounted for half its sales.

Introduction to the first edition
Nobody taught me nothing

I joined the London office of J. Walter Thompson Company
Limited in October 1954 and retired from it at the end of
December 1987. It was both the first proper job I ever had and
the last proper job I ever had.

On my first morning as a trainee copywriter I was given
something called a requisition by someone called a controller.
The requisition turned out to be a written request for some
words for an advertisement for Pan American World Airways,
and the controller was the traffic man who tried to make sure
things happened on time. The requisition stipulated that the
space to be filled was a six-inch double and the copy was
required for that day. I didn't know what a six-inch double
was, I knew nothing at all about Pan American World
Airways, and my boss was away ill.

Learning on the job is what you do in advertising agencies.
It is true that some good agencies, and J. Walter Thompson
was and is one of them, take training extremely seriously.
Courses and seminars are run and people are taught how to
work in teams, how to approach problems, how to make
media decisions, how to plan strategies. But learning on the
job is still what matters most.

You learn from everyone. You learn from your boss, from
your friends, from your enemies, from people in other
departments, from your clients and from your competitors.
You work a lot of it out for yourself – in fact this book might
have been called *Picking It Up As You Go Along*. Long before
you think you're ready, you will find yourself responsible for
other people. I think I learnt more from subordinates than I

ever did from superiors: you have to think harder when talking to them; you have to find words and principles to explain your instinctive reactions to their ideas.

Rather rumly, there aren't many helpful books to read. Of the few that there are, most make sense only after you've been doing the job for a year or two. The best that I know are by Claude Hopkins, David Ogilvy, Rosser Reeves and James Webb Young. Even more surprisingly, there are virtually no worthwhile videotapes.

It is perfectly possible for you to have a brilliant advertising idea on your first morning before lunch. (I didn't.) What is not possible at all is for you to know *why* it's a good idea. That's the skill that takes time to develop – and that's the bit that makes it difficult, and why it all continues to be both baffling and rewarding. Advertising people who fail to develop a curiosity about advertising – why it exists, how it works, what it does – invariably get bored and stale and, sooner or later, fired. It is often said of them that they've burnt themselves out, but the truth is that they never looked beneath the surface; and the surface of advertising can get very boring quite quickly.

All the pieces in this book were written for specific reasons over the last twenty years or so. Some were articles for the trade press; some for internal use; some were speeches or presentations. They all, in different ways, poke about a bit beneath the surface.

So you won't find anything much about *advertisements,* for example: how to write them, how to use music, how big the picture ought to be or whether cartoons are a Good Idea. And you won't find anything at all about the money side of advertising: how much you need to spend and where to spend it.

What I hope you will find are insights; some helpful thoughts and speculations about the nature of *advertising:* what it is, what it does, how it works, how it impinges on real life and how to make it happen. As dividers between these sections, I've included some other insights of a rather different kind, principally there to convey the flavour of working in an advertising agency; because it can be, and often is, a heady combination of pressure and bathos, achievement and absurdity. In 33 years, I never found it boring.

About the only disadvantage of staying with one agency all your working life is that you never work with your competitors. I am never certain if I like so many of them so much because they are intrinsically so likeable, or because I've never had to work with them.

One great and recent treat, through membership of the WPP Group board, has been the chance to get to know David Ogilvy. It has not been a disappointment. Not only has he written a most generous Foreword but he has also provided a title for this book. ('It suggests skulduggery and sex,' he wrote. If so, there will be disappointment.)

While it is true that nobody taught me nothing, some people taught me a lot more than others. Alphabetically these are Bernard Gutteridge, Stephen King, Denis Lanigan, Tom Sutton, Chris Thomas and John Treasure, all at J. Walter Thompson.

It was Ann Page, as my secretary, who started to keep the things I wrote. Without her thoughtfully invisible discipline, there would have been no book.

The thought of the book itself, together with many helpful suggestions, came from Harry Clark, and the time he has generously spent collecting material is greatly appreciated.

I am also much indebted to Terry Hamaton, who designed and drew the delightful illustrations for *The consumer has a mind as well as a stomach.*

My principal debt of gratitude must be to the corporate J. Walter Thompson: a remarkable advertising agency around the world. It gave me interest and income for 33 years; and even, as I left, the means by which the words of this introduction have been processed.

My tragic past

Written in 1977 as one of a series for Campaign *on 'How I Got Into Advertising'. It covers some of the same ground as* The case of the missing policeman *(page 220) but is a good deal more reliable factually. Slightly edited to avoid repetition.*

My father, who was a copywriter at Greenly's, started his own breakaway agency in the mid-1920s. It was called Bullmores Ltd. and was a founder member of the reconstituted Institute of Practitioners in Advertising in 1927. Soon afterwards his business went into liquidation. Disillusioned, he joined MI6 for whom he worked, off and on, until his death in mysterious circumstances in Calcutta in 1947.

My family was deeply scarred by this experience, and, although I was not born until 1929, I was brought up to believe that it was the advertising business that had brought ruin upon my father. As I grew older, I grew ever more determined to succeed where he had failed; to vindicate his reputation; to conquer the trade that had conquered him. And so it was, on leaving university in the early 1950s, that my only thought was to join an advertising agency and work my way up.

At this point I think I should reveal that, while the first paragraph above is factually true, the second paragraph (with the exception of my date of birth) is not.

I was dimly aware that my father had been in something called advertising, but since I never met him from the time I was five, and since my mother never spoke about him at all, advertising as a career seemed no more attractive to me, on the infrequent occasions when I thought about a career, than, say, agricultural engineering.

The only thing I was any good at at school was writing. I still experience a shiver of shame and triumph when I remember that I achieved a Distinction in Higher School Certificate (A-Levels to non-wrinklies) on the strength of a paper I wrote about six set books, none of which I'd read.

Because I was good at writing, I chose to read English when I arrived at Oxford. No one had told me that the English curriculum at Oxford was one-third Latin, one-third Anglo-Saxon and one-third the inhuman dissection of English Literature.

My tutor was J.I.M. Stewart, who still writes detective stories under the name of Michael Innes. On the top of my third essay he neatly pencilled the following encouraging comment: 'You can write; but remember, this can be something of a disadvantage in the study of the English language.'

So I stopped reading English at Oxford, although I didn't think to mention it to anyone, and I wrote a piece of verse for *Isis*. This featured three men then writing film reviews for the magazine. They were called Colin Curley, Derek Knight and Terence Twigg, and I was young enough to find their names funny. It wasn't very good, but everything that has happened to me since can be traced directly back to that one piece of verse.

I was asked to write more, and did. I was asked to write the annual revue for the Experimental Theatre Club, and did. I spent most of one vacation writing it instead of revising Books IV and VI of the *Aeneid* (if that's how it's spelt). The revue was staged in the summer term in a marquee pitched in the grounds of Merton College. I can't remember why.

The revue was a success but my third attempt at passing my Latin Preliminary Examination was not.

I telephoned Jim Stewart. 'I wonder,' I said, 'if you could tell me what my position is.'

'Well, Jeremy,' he said, then paused for several seconds, 'I don't think you've got one.'

So I went home to Norfolk, bred some ducks and studied *Punch* so that I could learn how to write the kind of humorous piece it might accept. I had just about mastered its preferred style when Malcolm Muggeridge took over as editor and the style changed. At about the same time, meat came off ration and nobody wanted to buy ducks. In the course of a few weeks, I'd learned two important lessons about marketing and communications.

But I did go on writing songs and sketches for the ETC, then under the leadership of Ned Sherrin, and would return furtively to Oxford to see them performed. In 1953, Ned took a company to Edinburgh, and this led to a shortened revue appearing on BBC television. Not many people can have seen this but George Butler did. George was then head of the art department at J. Walter Thompson and knew that something called commercial television was due to start in 1955. He wrote a letter to the BBC who passed it on to us. We'd never heard of J. Walter Thompson but Ned and I both needed jobs. I put on my blue suit and went off to be interviewed.

It very quickly became clear that George Butler had forgotten that he had ever written the letter. He pointed out that he ran the art department and that I couldn't draw. In 1954, art directors were required to draw.

As I stood up to go, relieved that this bizarre encounter was to be mercifully short-lived, George remembered that there was also something called the editorial department. That's what the copy department was called in 1954.

'Perhaps you should take the copy test,' he said, with more charity than conviction.

So I did. I was interviewed by Norman Bassett, head of the copy department, who told me about the Great Margarine War; and by a psychologist, who asked me what I thought about a series of obscene ink-blots.

Months passed. By this time, another version of the revue, unhappily titled *Oxford Accents,* was appearing at a very small underground theatre called the Watergate, off the Strand. That was all Watergate meant in 1954.

Kenneth Tynan panned it. I was paid £12 for the six-week run, and I still needed a job.

Eventually I was summoned from a gliding course in Dunstable and offered £10 a week to start as a trainee copywriter. It was pointed out that the offer would have been more generous had I been a graduate.

Gratefully I accepted, amazed that anyone should pay me to do anything. When I discovered that what I was required to do was totally absorbing and infinite in its variety, my amazement increased. It's still with me.

1
What advertising is

Advertising: what is it?

Most discussion about advertising's social and economic effect is conducted as though all advertising is designed, almost conspiratorially, to have a uni-directional influence. I first tried to point out the distinction between *advertising* and *advertisements* in a J. Walter Thompson London publication in 1975. I tried again when asked to write this introduction to the *Advertising Association Handbook* in 1983. (I am credited with having helped edit it; in fact, Mike Waterson did it all.) Whenever an occasion arose – and often when it didn't – I went on trying to make the distinction but have yet, to my knowledge, to convince anyone of its validity. Either I'm wrong or the continued confusion suits lazy-minded pundits. The piece contains a definition of advertising which has found its way, not always without challenge, into several standard advertising books. Winston Fletcher, probably rightly, thinks he's got a better one.

Almost as many claims have been made about advertising as advertising makes about products. A small selection might include:

> Advertising is evil
>
> Advertising exploits human inadequacy
>
> Advertising is wasteful
>
> Advertising is the mainspring of the economy
>
> Advertising prevents small, enterprising companies from breaking into established markets
>
> Advertising is a force for change

A moment's reflection is enough to make one realise that each of these statements, favourable and unfavourable alike, is a generalisation directly equivalent to a statement such as 'Television makes children violent.'

Some television *programmes* may make children violent; some may help them learn to read. Some *advertisements* may be wasteful; some may act as a force for change, but as I hope to show, not all advertisements can possibly have identical effects.

Advertising is simply one of many available channels of communication. It is available, at a price, to everyone – and allows people to make contact with one or more other people for an almost infinite number of different ends. *Advertisements* are the messages that advertising carries, in an attempt to achieve those ends.

The almost infinite number of different users, uses, aims, purposes, motives, audiences, media and methods makes the question 'What is advertising?' peculiarly difficult to answer. The sign outside a church naming next Sunday's preacher is an advertisement. So are these:

> Locally Grown Strawberries
>
> We Need 175 Mountain Commandos
>
> Rights Issue
>
> Chairman's Statement
>
> Lost Budgerigar
>
> Labour Isn't Working
>
> Confessions Of A Pop Performer (X)
>
> Britain Will Win With Labour
>
> Broad-minded Midland-based Male Seeks Mature Relationship
>
> Could You Manage An Off-Licence?
>
> Save It!
>
> Cats Will Die Unless We Continue To Help Them

These are all advertisements and they are all part of advertising.

The nearest I can get to a definition which encompasses all these possible differences is: 'Any paid-for communication intended to inform and/or influence one or more people'.

First: 'paid-for'. An advertisement that is not paid for is not an advertisement, though its cost may be minimal and the payment may not be to a media owner.

Second: 'communication'. Every advertisement is attempting to bridge a gap between a sender and one or more potential receivers. That bridge is a form of communication. To buy a 16-sheet poster site and leave it absolutely blank is not to advertise. There must, in other words, be content as well as medium.

Third: 'intended'. Not all advertisements 'work', in the sense of achieving their desired objectives, but they are nonetheless part of advertising.

Fourth: 'inform and/or influence'. The purely informative advertisement may be rare and the distinction between information and persuasion may be difficult to draw (what about 'Gratuities Not Included' on a British Rail breakfast bill, for example?), but an advertisement does not have to set out to influence either attitude or behaviour in order to qualify.

And finally: 'one or more people'. All advertisements are addressed to people: sometimes one ('Gypsy. Am back. Call soon. Lollipop') and sometimes millions ('Don't Waste Water').

Some years ago, a lady in Dulwich decided that she no longer needed her second-hand electric riding camel so she bought a space in the *Times*. This space was filled with an advertisement which was in turn read by one or more other people, previously unknown to the lady from Dulwich, who happened to want a second-hand electric riding camel and were well prepared to pay £400 o.n.o. to get one. The lucky applicant was happy; the lady from Dulwich was happy; the *Times* was happy; the *Times*' readers were happy (since the insertion cost helped to pay for their newspaper); and the second-hand electric riding camel found itself once more both wanted and useful.

Exactly the same simple principle applies to the Department of Energy, when it wants us to conserve energy; to the Prudential, when it wants to recruit personnel for its pensions and administration departments; to the Home Office, when it wants us to keep matches away from children; to a foreign government that feels itself to be misunderstood and wants to put its case; and to Heinz, when it wants to make clear the virtues of its baby foods to millions of parents it's never met.

All these advertisers have just this in common: they wanted to achieve something and chose advertising as one means of achieving it. How they used that advertising, the advertisements themselves, varied enormously in style, intent, format, price, size and medium. Whether or not they were as satisfied with the results of their expenditure as the lady from Dulwich, only they will know. So to attempt to identify some shared and general purpose or effect in all those advertisements is manifestly absurd.

'Is advertising wasteful?' is a non-question since 'are advertisements wasteful?' can be answered only by the person who paid for each one and sometimes not even then.

Was the Dulwich lady's advertisement wasteful? Demonstrably not. (Alas, the cost-effectiveness of other advertisements is much less easy to demonstrate.) But it would have been wasteful had her electric riding camel rotted away in its Dulwich attic, unknown to all those who were longing to acquire it. In other words, it would have been wasteful *not* to advertise.

By substituting 'advertisements' for 'advertising', equivalent points can be made about all the statements at the beginning of this chapter, and many more besides.

Do advertisements prevent small, enterprising companies from breaking into established markets? Ask Polaroid or Bernard Matthews.

Are advertisements a force for change? Ask the manufacturers of those brand leaders that have continued to lead their markets for 30, 40 years or more.

Advertising, as such, can do absolutely nothing. It is simply there, waiting to be used. Advertisements, in theory, can do practically everything: introduce the new, confirm the old, congratulate existing buyers/users/consumers/employees, or attempt to convert them. Advertisements can, and do, encourage consumption and encourage thrift, and advocate a vote for any number of competing brands, companies or political parties.

Television, as we have seen, suffers from the same semantic confusion. Like advertising, it is simply an available channel of communication: there are cameras, transmitters and receivers. How can these inoffensive and inanimate pieces of hardware, of themselves, encourage violence? (Except, of course, by failing to function.)

It is both legitimate and healthy to question the effect of television programmes, just as it is to question the effect of certain advertisements, but to suggest that advertising does this or television does that is nonsense.

In fact, one of the few commercially available channels of communication not to suffer from this confusion between the container and the thing contained is the telephone system. Some subscribers use the telephone to sell insurance policies; some to call the plumber; some to say 'How are you?'; some to get in touch with the Samaritans; and some, no doubt, to arrange for the collection of a new consignment of hard drugs. Some unhappy subscribers use the telephone for breathing down heavily and saying 'knickers'. Again, the same channel of communication is being used for an infinite number of different purposes, including, sadly, some undeniable abuses.

However, because no one ever confuses the telephone system with telephone conversations, we have, so far at least, been spared the suggestion that radical reforms and controls are required in order to prevent one man in a raincoat from saying 'knickers', however understandably distressed the receiver of that message might be.

The distinction between advertising and advertisements is clear, and it's been made many times before by many people. Yet somehow it always seems to get forgotten in the heat of commercial, social and political thundering.

This handbook seeks, among other things, to spell out in some detail the diversity of the industry so often thought of as one homogeneous whole, as witnessed by phrases of the 'advertising is ...' sort. It seeks to show the great diversity of the media and the great diversity of types of advertiser. It attempts to spell out the role of the advertising agency in producing effective advertising. It touches on the role of advertising in the economy, on some sensitive issues in advertising, on advertising controls, and on public attitudes to advertising.

As co-editor, my one great hope for this book is that having looked at even part of it, the reader will never again feel inclined to say 'advertising is ...'.

Competitive persuasion

In the 1950s and 1960s, at least among the chattering classes as they were to become known, both 'competition' and 'persuasion' were pretty dirty words. Vance Packard's *The Hidden Persuaders* was published in 1957; and though most people neglected to read the book, the title alone entitled them to agree with it. I first came across the phrase 'competitive persuasion' in a paper written by John Brunner when he was on the *Observer*. It was, I believe, part of that paper's submission to the Shawcross Commission on the Press – which would date it 1961. The piece below was first written for JWT *in Britain 1978* and was reprinted in *Campaign* later that year.

We come to most of our decisions in this country as a result of what has been called 'the principle of competitive persuasion'.

As voters, we are offered the choice of more than one candidate, more than one political party. All parties, all candidates, have not only the right but the responsibility to put their cases to us as convincingly, as competitively and as persuasively as they can. We listen, we note, we compare and when it's time to vote, we make a choice.

The reasons for that choice are almost certain to be complex. Indeed, in the strict sense of the word, they may not be 'reasons' at all. Our choice may be influenced by habit, inertia, background, self-interest, political or social principle, misconception, prejudice, distaste for the alternatives – or a marvellously muddled combination of them all. But that's our privilege. It's our vote, and we can spend it as we wish.

As readers we are offered the choice of more than one newspaper, each in turn trying to persuade us not only of its own merits but of the merits of different ways of life and alternative governments. And again, we read, absorb, reject, modify – and make up our own minds.

As jurors we are offered the two alternative and often irreconcilable views of prosecution and defence. Again, we listen, discuss – and come to a conclusion.

The priceless value of this principle of competitive persuasion can be fully recognised only when we examine attempts to improve on it. If we try to eliminate 'wasteful' competition, or to save people from 'illogical' choices, we move rapidly towards authoritarianism and then on to totalitarianism.

Our television companies are required, by Charter and by Acts of Parliament, to observe what is called 'balance'. Well-intentioned though it undoubtedly was, the impracticality of this requirement becomes daily more apparent. Television programmes, like newspapers, are made by people – which is to say, subjective, passionate, differing, opinionated, fallible individuals. And it is inconceivable that the producers of programmes on property development or social benefits should, as individuals, remain genuinely neutral however hard they might try. Yet that seems to be what is expected of them because they are regarded not as individuals but as representatives of their companies.

Any serious programme, despite earnest and often comically contrived attempts to preserve 'balance', is likely to excite cries of outrage from at least one interested party because the reception of any communication is inevitably subjective: so much so that it is quite possible for all political parties, simultaneously, to believe that the BBC is joined in a conspiracy against them.

Not only does 'balance' not work, it's also potentially dangerous. If we are led to believe that because television programmes are balanced they express the truth, our critical faculties will be less alert. We may be tempted to think: 'It must be true, it was on television.'

It has long been fashionable to mock party political broadcasts – and it's certainly true that as pieces of communication, as examples of advocacy, they are frequently inept and occasionally, one would suspect, downright counterproductive. But at least, as viewers, we are left in no doubt as to their stance and their purpose. They are clearly labelled, unashamedly biased, with no pretensions to 'balance'. Balance is achieved not within broadcasts but, by strict allocation of time, between broadcasts. And it is up to each party to use its allocation of time as skilfully and persuasively as possible.

The same is true of conventional, paid-for advertising. Each advertisement is clearly seen to be an advertisement – or should be. This is why advertisements that do their best to look like editorial are quite properly prohibited by the codes of advertising practice.

As receivers of advertisements, we know that the advertiser is trying to put his own case as effectively as possible. But almost without exception, every advertiser, whether he's the manufacturer of branded goods or the Royal Air Force advertising for recruits, is in competition with other advertisers. So we can listen, compare, absorb, modify, reject, accept – and reach our own conclusions. The principle of competitive persuasion is at work again.

There are, however, some people and some bodies who seem to want to introduce into advertising the equivalent of 'balance' in broadcasting. Just as well-intentioned, they want to protect us from our own instincts, our own freedom to spend our money as we spend our vote. They want to apply their own standards to everyone; to add more and more controls to what an advertiser says and how he says it; to aim for greater 'truth' in advertising.

This trend, as with attempts at 'balance', is at best foolish, at worst dangerous.

Certainly, no man should be allowed to advertise a non-existent cottage in Cornwall, keep the deposits and disappear – but there's more than enough legislation to cope with him already. Other advertisers, whether rogues teetering on the brink of the law or those who make a mistake, are dealt with through a vigorous system of self-regulation. But some of the more extreme consumerists want to go beyond that. They believe that the principle of competitive persuasion leads to a cynical, sceptical society and that advertising that is more 'truthful' (in their terms) would be in everyone's interest.

I believe the opposite to be the case. I believe that competitive persuasion leads to a discriminating, alert, intelligent society in which each member can arrive at his or her own decisions – whether or not they seem rational, sensible and correct to any self-appointed protector.

Further, I believe that – while we should make every effort to check our facts and ensure that our advertisements are honest – we should be pleased rather than worried that people question the 'truthfulness' of advertising. They are acute enough to recognise that the essence of competitive persuasion lies in promise, hyperbole, emotion and all the other time-honoured techniques of rhetoric. Should the time ever come – which it won't – when everybody believes implicitly in every party political broadcast and every commercial advertisement, I for one would want to leave not only the business but the country.

The truth of the matter is that people enjoy being persuaded, being courted, been wooed, being wanted.

We may, as individuals, find certain advertisements irrelevant, boring, offensive, silly, extravagant and antisocial. Indeed, it's inevitable.

If a large number of people share that view, and they also happen to be the very people to whom the advertisement is addressed, then it's clearly a bad advertisement. But any damage that is done, is done not to the consumer but to the advertiser.

Every client we have is in competition with other advertisers. Every client we have is trying to improve his product or service, to tailor it more accurately to the needs of its ultimate users, and to promote it honestly and persuasively.

Win or lose, competition and competitive persuasion are in the interests of everyone in the country; and it remains a delight to be part of that process.

Why the Queen Mother was left in the dark under a street lamp

Marketing, August 1995

Stanley Resor bought J. Walter Thompson from J. Walter Thompson in 1916 and ran it until he retired in 1961. It's a great shame that the Poet Laureate never met him, but I did.

He gave me a whole hour of his time and he told me this story. A man was walking one night down a street in New York when he came across another man, on his hands and knees, under a street lamp. So the passer-by stopped, as you would in those days, and asked if he could help. And the man looked up and said, that would be kind, he'd dropped a dime. For several minutes they were both on their knees, sweeping their hands across the sidewalk under the street lamp, until the passer-by said: 'Well, I don't know. Are you absolutely certain you dropped it here?' And the man said: 'Oh no, dear me, no. I dropped it over there.' The passer-by, wiping the pigeon-droppings from his palms, not unreasonably said: 'Then why, might I ask, are you looking here?' And the man said: 'The light's better here.'

And because I was young and a foreigner and knew nothing about advertising, Mr Resor kindly went on to explain to me the meaning of this parable.

Not all products were intrinsically interesting, he said, so it was the job of the advertising agency to make them so. If you took the easy way out, you would go to where the light was, leaving the dime in the dark. And that, said Mr Resor in 1958, was the reason for a lot of irrelevant advertising. Distinctive, possibly: but distinction without relevance was of no value to the advertiser and evidence of gross unprofessionalism on the part of his agency. What we were paid to do, he said, was to bring the light to the dime: and that was why advertising was so difficult.

Had Ted Hughes met Mr Resor, he might well have declined the invitation to become Poet Laureate. If you're a free-spirited poet, you may – indeed, you must – start where the light is. You do not have to write unless a subject appeals to you. But if you're the Poet Laureate, you're like a journeyman copywriter. Somebody gives you both a brief and a deadline: kindly write something flattering about this cook-in sauce or this elderly royal person, and may we have it by early August, please?

In other words, Poets Laureate, like agency creative teams, have to start with the dime. And that, as Mr Resor knew and Ted Hughes must now be finding out, is difficult. This month, the Poet Laureate's dime was the Queen Mother; and his tribute to her 95th birthday got a right roasting.

The Crown should learn from the past. Because visual irrelevance is far harder to mock than verbal, we should de-commission the Poet Laureate for good; and instead, whenever inconsequential national events demand, commission a painting. Agencies, denied this escape route, will have to go on trying to do the difficult thing.

Whatever happened to the Hidden Persuaders?

Marketing, January 1997

The most famous book about advertising is not about advertising. Vance Packard published *The Hidden Persuaders* in 1957 and his death last month at the age of 82 prompted me to read it again.

At the time he wrote it, a great economic change was taking place in America.

Noted by theologians as well as economists, the new age of abundance was turning the long-standing relationship of production and consumption upside-down. Until then, it had been the accepted responsibility of production to satisfy demand. Now, quite suddenly it seemed, it had become the responsibility of demand to absorb production.

This reversal of roles created a need for marketing men. Packard calls them merchandisers. Their job was to create competitive demand for increasingly similar competitive products – and to do that, they needed to acquire a deeper, richer understanding of the relationship that existed between products and consumers. And in order to do *that*, they needed help: which came from a bunch of entrepreneurial psychologists and social scientists who called themselves motivational researchers.

These are the hidden persuaders of the title. Most of them were not only doctors or professors but also had sinister foreign names: Ernest Dichter, PhD, was their high priest. What they did was *depth* research: they raided the privacy of people's minds so that they could, allegedly, more easily (and subconsciously) be persuaded to buy more of what they didn't need. Traditional researchers could tell you what people *said* they thought. Motivational researchers told you what people *really* thought (even if they didn't know it themselves).

In his three-paragraph introduction to the British Pelican edition, Packard uses the word 'manipulate' or a derivative four times. The publisher's note warns: 'the frightening processes evolved and applied by American super-advertising scientists are having an increasing effect upon the potential victims in Britain.'

This scary-science card is used to great effect. Dr Dichter ran the Institute for Motivational Research. One chapter talks of the psycho-seduction of children. Spooky references are made to Minnesota multi-phasic personality inventories, Rorschach and Thematic Apperception Tests, hypnosis, and Cassirer's epistemology of symbolic forms.

Oddly, subliminal advertising (the rumours of which did so much for Packard's sales, and which many people believe the book to be about) is not mentioned; there's just a single, dismissive reference to something called 'sub-threshold effects'.

In fact, without knowing it, the book describes the first fumbling attempts to distinguish brands from products. (Gardner and Levy were themselves motivational researchers; their 'The Product and the Brand' had been published in the *Harvard Business Review* in 1955.) Reading the book again, it seems clear that Packard himself was not greatly alarmed by his own revelations: he found the merchandising process fascinating and largely innocent. The language, and above all the title, were there to persuade us (subconsciously, of course) to buy the book.

And we did. Few, I suspect, read it. But with a title like that, you think you don't have to.

The hair restorer that didn't

In 1974, The Advertising Association held one of its most memorable conferences. Hostility to advertising was running high, at least in political circles, and the conference was addressed by both Shirley Williams as Consumer Affairs Minister and the first Director General of Fair Trading, John Methven. Both made clear their doubts about the efficacy of current voluntary advertising controls. Ronnie Kirkwood enlisted my help in a presentation he had been invited to make at the same conference (see also *The case of the missing policeman*, page 220) and we chose, perhaps riskily, to adopt a satirical approach. The following is a short excerpt from the speech. It recounts an entirely fictional future event – but the argument is much the same as that contained in *Competitive persuasion* (page 19).

In 1999, a manufacturer called Rebozo Laboratories ran an advertisement for a hair product called Pom. The illustration was of a markedly balding man and the text read: '*GOING BALD? New Pom can help arrest hair loss.*'

Although this claim was fairly muted and qualified, it was still demonstrably a lie. Under controlled clinical conditions, with a volunteer panel of 1,000 balding men, it was found that the 500 using Pom lost no less hair than the 500 using massage alone. Furthermore, although the product was described as 'new', it was established that there had been no significant change in formulation for 13 years.

It was a blatant example of a manufacturer playing on the concerns and neuroses of a particular group of people and deliberately attempting to mislead them into believing his product could do something he knew perfectly well it could not. The advertisement was withdrawn and Rebozo Laboratories were very properly fined a great deal of money.

And there the matter might have rested had it not attracted the attention of Alexander Morrison, then Professor of Communications at Redruth University. Professor Morrison was a leading authority on communications theory and had been watching the development of advertising controls with keen professional interest.

His own view, unfashionable at the time, was that consumer protectionists, with whose aims he greatly sympathised, were nevertheless extremely naive in their view of how communications actually worked – and he decided to use the case of the hair restorer in an experiment of his own.

The first thing he did was to prepare a new version of the irresponsible advertisement.

He kept the illustration of the balding man exactly as it was and he kept the headline exactly as it was – but he took out the offending copy altogether so the advertisement simply read: *'GOING BALD?'* No copy, no claim – just a picture of the product. And he tested this version for communication and persuasion using the original advertisement – the one that had explicitly claimed to arrest hair loss – as a control.

What he found in no way surprised him. The original advertisement still misled: a substantial number of men was led to expect that Pom might prevent their loss of hair continuing. But his new version, the one which claimed absolutely nothing, was significantly *more* misleading. Indeed, a large number of men interpreted it as promising not just a reduction in the rate of hair *loss* but actual *restoration*. Encouraged by this finding, Professor Morrison went one stage further and produced yet another version of the ad.

Again the same illustration of the balding man was used, but this time the copy read: *'GOING BALD? New enriched Pom guarantees you a completely new head of hair in just five minutes!'*

Again he tested this for communication and persuasion against the original, and again his findings failed to surprise him. The original continued to mislead as before – *but his third version misled absolutely nobody.* It was instantly and totally repudiated by his panel, not one of whom said he would ever be tempted to try it.

Professor Morrison published the results of his experiment in an article in *Communications Today*. He conceded that the third version had been deliberately extreme and therefore to some extent unrealistic. But he pointed out the apparent paradox that an advertisement which said absolutely nothing, and which was therefore legal, could mislead the consumer not only more than the original but a great deal more than the third version which contained blatant lies and unsubstantiable claims and was therefore totally illegal. As he put it himself: 'Here is a proven instance where the consumer is in fact far better protected by a demonstrable lie than by an unclaimed truth.'

Being a man who enjoyed encouraging controversy and challenging accepted wisdom, he went on to suggest that to require all advertising to be decent, legal and truthful was in fact acting against the interests of the consumer. In a memorable last paragraph he wrote: 'Indeed, there is a growing body of evidence to suggest that the consumer would most actively be protected by insisting that all advertising be *untruthful* at least in certain demonstrable respects, and that fact should be widely known and understood by the public at large.'

The 60-ft peacock in Times Square: a role model for the networks

Marketing, February 1996

Any time now, the Nissin Food Products Company Ltd of Tokyo will unveil a new advertisement for Nissin Cup Noodles.

Dominating the north face of Number One Times Square, it will be 60 ft high, employ prodigious quantities of red neon, live steam and animated noodle, and will cost $1 million to install and another $130,000 a month to expose.

Those who believe that modern, accountable media planning should deliver a measurable audience composed exclusively of solus users will disapprove. How can a single poster site, reaching an unknown audience, not one of whom may be a cup noodle groupie, conceivably deliver a pay-back on $2.5 million?

For years, I've been haughtily disparaging about the terms 'classified' and 'display'. A far more useful way to think of advertising, I've argued, is to distinguish between advertising that people consciously go out and look for; and advertising that consciously goes out and looks for people.

All classified advertising, of course, belongs to the first category – and so, it seems, will much of the new media advertising. www advertising doesn't come looking for you; you choose to go looking for it.

But the kind of advertising that is most valuable to brands is the kind of advertising that is least likely to be sought after by people.

Brand advertising has to draw attention to itself. If it's skilfully done, it will be at worst tolerated and at best warmly received; but it is never an invited guest. People don't go out for a nice drive of a Sunday afternoon to catch up on the new posters. They don't say: 'You know, Cheryl, I rather fancy we've fallen behind on our Ariel ad intake recently. Let's stay at home this evening and take some in.' Brand advertising has to go out looking for people; that's why it attracts all the criticism and that's why it's difficult to do well.

All of which has belatedly made me wonder if the origin of the word 'display' may not be typographical after all, but zoological: '*Display – a pattern of behaviour by which the animal attracts attention while courting.*' Even if it isn't, it should be. What better inspiration for your creative team than a peacock of unbounded vanity, spreading and parading its multi-coloured magnificence in the face of some indifferent peahen – with the prospect of a right good consummation as the reward for success?

The Nissin cup noodle sign will be *on display* in Times Square. Twenty million people a year will take photographs of it. Millions of postcards will celebrate it. Documentaries and feature films will give it, for nothing, further glamour and distribution. Nissin cup noodles will become a famous global brand on the strength of a single poster.

Fame, by its very nature, is indiscriminate – so only mass media can deliver it. The real competition for traditional mass media will come not from the Internet but from other magnificent forms of indiscriminate display: stunts, sponsorship, round-the-world balloon trips and 60-ft peacocks in Times Square.

[1998 note: the Internet, of course, carries both kinds of advertising. Much of it people actively choose to look for, but banner advertising attempts to ambush the browser in much the same way as the giant peacock. As a private medium, however, it still lacks the ability to create indiscriminate fame.]

Two hot tips: beware Barnum, remember Ratner

Marketing, October 1997

It was probably Phineas T. Barnum who said that all publicity is good publicity. For showmen it may be good advice. And as long as you don't think about it too carefully, it's not bad advice generally. These days, modern marketing directors and their sophisticated advertising agencies tend to under-rate the solid commercial value of crude fame. They're so busy calibrating some miniscule shift in brand-positioning on their Boston Grids that the good old-fashioned benefits of familiarity and brand celebrity get lost in the detail. Most publicity, more often than not, is mostly good. But that is not what Barnum said.

As always, what every hypothesis demands is challenge. So if someone presents you with the Barnum hypothesis, I suggest you look them straight in the face and say 'Ratner!'

Poor old Gerald generated so much free publiciity for himself and his shops that they took away his job and had to change the company's trading name. I do not think Gerald Ratner would agree with Phineas T. Barnum.

It's been said that Peter Mandelson deliberately raised his public profile during the summer in the belief that the massive publicity would carry him shoulder-high on to the NEC. Even more recently, Tony Banks has become far better known than he's ever been, with terminal implications for his political career.

Watergate, Lockerbie, Hoover, Brent Spar: some publicity is bad publicity.

With the inevitable and continuing trend away from traditional free-standing brands towards corporate brands and service brands, all this becomes a lot more important. Parent brands, master brands, company brands will need lots of simple salience, lots of familiarity, lots of well-knownness. But when a corporate reputation takes a nasty knock, the effects are impossible to contain completely; they can sweep like a virus through the entire enterprise. If you stick to your policy of free-standing brands, damage limitation is relatively easy. Tylenol can be kept in an isolation ward while the rest of Johnson & Johnson carries on trading. Corporate branding makes that impossible.

So at a time when the value of simple publicity is due for rediscovery, when event marketing and sponsorship and joint ventures are attracting increasing interest and investment, and when corporate reputations are being asked to extend their authority over an ever greater diversity of goods and services, the word Ratner should be in pokerwork above every chief executive's desk: not as a deterrent but as a reminder.

Publicity is not just a cheaper form of advertising: it is different in kind. You should not assume you can control it. It's not that difficult to get a flame started but you can never be sure of being able to douse it. Unlike advertising, publicity can kill.

To act as though all publicity was good publicity is to be one of those who, also according to Phineas T. Barnum, are born every minute.

Why soft-sell is hard to sell: it isn't selling

Marketing, May 1996

Here's a bit of a puzzle, then. Everybody agrees that hard-sell and soft-sell are pretty meaningless phrases, yet everybody goes on using them.

They seem to be most favoured by those believing that the only true paradigm for advertising is the hi-performance brain-invader, by which something called a consumer proposition is rifled repetitively into consumers' heads until they can play it back flawlessly to day-after recallers. This, approvingly, is called hard-sell. Anything else, disapprovingly, is called soft-sell. (These are the same people who complain that a commercial is insufficiently branded, when what they really mean is that the product name has only featured five times.)

If that was all there was to it – hard, good; soft, bad – the deadly phrases would have expired long ago.

But there's another distinction they're sometimes used to make which is a good deal more useful: and it's mainly to do with different kinds of immediacy. If you want your audience to do something soon – cut a coupon, send a fax, pick up a phone, go to a sale – then you'll probably want to be sharp and urgent. These qualities are not sympathetic. They can be strident. They may not add long-term value to your brand. And you may not care.

But if the purpose of your advertising is to charge your brand's batteries, to add to its warmth and desirability, to remind existing users of its presence and its purpose, then you'll be looking for another kind of immediacy: of connection rather than action. Urgency, with its attendant stridency, will be unwanted and unwise. You'll need to be well-mannered.

Depending on whether it's a real one or not, there are two good ways to sell a Rolex. The first is from a dodgy barrow on Oxford Street with the punters passing at walking speed. You have 15 seconds to get them before you lose them. The price is low enough to tempt them and high enough to make them hesitate. You do not pause to calculate possible damage to long-term brand values and corporate reputation. You will never see these punters again. You will hit them hard.

And the other way to sell a Rolex is the way they sell real ones in real life: politely and assuredly, with a style and grace to match the merchandise; conscious, as always, that every advertisement should be making a small investment in the brand's eternal worth.

The first approach is hard, the second soft. The second is far more difficult to do. But in meeting their own quite different objectives, they are comparably effective. Marketing needs both.

In fact, of course, the villain word is neither hard nor soft but sell. Sell implies that you're after an immediate, directly linked transaction; yet a great deal of advertising is not. A great deal of advertising is maintaining brand relevance and brand value.

So 'sell' favours hard but not soft. Hard-sell sounds muscular and commercial; and soft-sell sounds weedy and a contradiction in terms. But I bet we all go on using them.

On quality

Perhaps because I find difficulty in adding up, and have never been able to do long division, I have lived most of my life cowering away from figures in an undignified confusion of contempt and deference. It was liberating to begin to realise that numbers are just as unreliable as words – and all the more so for seeming not to be. The piece that follows started out in 1984 as an after-dinner speech at a Tower Housewares conference, at which I'd been asked to talk about Quality and Design, and it became the basis for a short introduction later the same year to the Advertising Association conference in London. This version, here edited slightly to avoid duplication, appeared in the *International Journal of Advertising* in 1985.

Why was it, some 30 years ago, that three Englishmen, Chris Chataway, Chris Brasher and Roger Bannister, ran round and round a fairly small dirt track in Oxford to the limits of physical and mental endurance? Quite simply, because a measurement existed. In fact, to be more precise, *two* measurements: one of distance and one of time. The point where those two measurements met had been called a barrier and had become a challenge. Yet, if you come to think of it, the barrier was based on the arbitrary collision of two arbitrary numbers.

Four minutes is no more nor less than 240 seconds and has no greater intrinsic interest or value than 239 or 252 seconds. And a *mile* is even more ridiculous. I'll tell you what a mile is: it's 1,760 yards. So what is a yard? Well, a yard is made up of three things called feet. And a foot? Well that's what you get when you add 12 inches together. So now we're getting near the truth. The moment we know what an inch is, we'll know what a mile is. Look up the definition of an inch in a dictionary and what do you find? 'One-twelfth of a linear foot.' Which, as definitions go, seems to me a trifle on the circular side.

However, none of this bothered Messrs Chataway, Brasher and Bannister. They (and the whole world, including me) accepted those two wholly arbitrary measurements as having importance, devoted years of their lives to beating them and have been remembered for it ever since. And quite right, too. But just consider this. Had Bannister run 1,770 yards in four minutes and one second it would have been an even more remarkable performance but nobody would have known how to talk about it.

Numbers are both our obsession and our security blanket. They fascinate us, and they provide the rules for the games we like to play: which of course explains the success of the *Guinness Book of Records*. And, by success, I mean of course the number of copies sold. So I'm quantifying again.

Company chairmen, in their annual statements, use numbers, both lavishly and quite often very creatively. Unless it's convenient, little if any notice is taken of inflation; so 'yet another record year' means that a company made less money in real terms than it did in 1969. We were told recently that the *FT* index had broken the 1,000 barrier for the first time. Few commentators bothered to point out that, for the *FT* index to have achieved a *real* new level, it would have had to reach 3,000. We not only love numbers but love to delude ourselves with numbers. They *feel* absolute, even when we know they're not.

I think part of our infatuation with quantity stems from our unease in dealing with quality. High quality, as we all know, is desirable, but how can you recognise it? If you could *measure* quality, that would be marvellous; but – Catch 22 – if you could, then it wouldn't be quality.

This fact, however, does not stop us from trying. Who is the most beautiful girl in the world? An absurd and unanswerable question. Yet the winner of the Miss World competition is invariably described in that way, and earns millions of dollars, pounds and francs being presented as such. Abruptly, however,

12 months later, she stops being the most beautiful girl in the world and someone else takes over. And consider, too, how quantifying quality is itself quantified: she's invariably described as being 34-21-34, or thereabouts. (And may I remind you that having a 34-inch chest means that your chest is 34 times one-twelfth of a linear foot – and that's all it means.)

Is Mrs Thatcher more or less popular with the Conservative Party than she was last year? Another difficult question, since it demands opinion and judgment. Or does it? It has become a habit now at party conferences for the applause at the end of the leader's speech to be *timed* in length and *measured* by decibel strength. Thus we *know* (because we have numbers) that Dr David Owen is a better leader than Mr Roy Jenkins.

When companies plan a major feature film production, they tend to add the population of the United Kingdom to the population of the United States in the belief that a movie with appeal to 300 million people will be better than one with appeal to 56 million. (Better, in the sense of taking more money at the box-office: yet another quantification often used to imply quality.)

Hence adventures such as *Raise the Titanic*. When told of the losses that the film had incurred, the remarkable Lew Grade is alleged to have said: 'Jesus Christ. It'd have been cheaper to lower the Atlantic.'

The makers of *Chariots of Fire* made no such calculation, or, if they did, they ignored it. They made what they believed would be a *good* film: and millions of people round the world agreed with them. Yet the budget for *Chariots* (yet another quantification) was a fraction of the budget for *Raise the Titanic*.

Because price is a number, we can compare prices with a pleasing precision. £2.75 is 25p less than £3.00. What we find harder to compare is *value*: while price is objective and universal, value is subjective and rated by each individual.

'Pile it high and sell it cheap', said the late Jack Cohen; and it served him well for a very long time. But as people in this country got richer – properly richer, not just inflation-richer – it served him less well. Sainsbury's (to simplify wildly) said, 'Yes, of course, price is important: but price for *what?*' And it made *judgments* about quality and the standards it demanded; and customers responded with gratitude (which you can't measure) and cash (which you can). It would seem that Woolworths has still not broken the habit of taking into account only those factors which can be quantified.

A question which continues to defy all attempts at quantification is of course individual financial reward. How much do people deserve to be paid? How much are they worth? And here again the potency of numbers is only too evident. Once any mention has been made of a five per cent 'norm', that five per cent becomes a fixed minimum in the minds of those negotiating for more. To a man or woman who negotiates income individually, salary is more than money: it's a measurement, a quantification, of how much they are loved, regarded and appreciated, both absolutely and relatively. Who believes any wage or salary structure is just and equitable? (If you do, you're a very remarkable group.) Company titles serve as some sort of public statement of a person's worth; and being hierarchical, they are close in kind to numbers. But most of us need both. A qualitative assessment at the end of a year can be welcome (if favourable), but it doesn't have the demonstrable, concrete, measurable effect of a rise.

So, if we aren't conscious of the danger, that which we can measure takes precedence over that which we can't. Numbers can deceive: they appear to be absolute, but they aren't. The Government can justifiably claim to have a 144-seat majority in the House of Commons, which is true. This can lead them – and others who should know better – to believe that the Government has overwhelming support in the country. It hasn't: well under half the country voted for them at the last election. They enjoyed greater popular support in 1979, when their *Parliamentary* majority was far less. The numbers deceive; and the results can be dangerous, not least because our leaders, like ourselves, are very selective in the numbers they choose to believe.

With all this obsession with numbers, what suffers? Lew Grade found out, Tesco found out, the travel industry found out, Woolworths may find out. What suffers is quality. What goes undervalued is judgment, talent, worth, intuition, instinct, vision, inventiveness.

If 'quality' is a slippery, elusive word, so is the word 'design'. Sometimes we use it to mean aesthetics or visual appeal, as in 'interior designer'. And sometimes we use it in a totally functional sense, as in 'design flaw'.

Last year, the magazine *Design,* published by the Design Centre, ran an article entitled 'Design and the Age of Quality'. It begins like this:

'Today, a growing number of manufacturing companies see product quality as the key to competitive success. For years, priority was given to reducing costs, first by controlling wages and inflation, latterly by the introduction of new technology and automation. But just when new technology has made it feasible to match the low retail prices of overseas competitors, the rules of the game have changed. Consumers have switched the emphasis of their priorities from price to quality and value – a change manufacturers have been slow to spot and find hard to deal with.'

The authors offered no evidence for this broad assertion, so I feel equally free to challenge some parts of it.

I do not, myself, believe that 'consumers have switched the emphasis of their priorities from price to quality and value'. I believe that consumers have *always* wanted quality and value. The factor of price (which is measurable) has been, and will remain, a negative, restricting factor in the sense that, however much I may want something, if I haven't got the money, I can't buy it. Low price, *as such*, is seldom a positive incentive to choose. There are very few consumer markets in this country where the cheapest brand is also the brand leader.

This quibble doesn't damage the basis of the authors' argument. It does, however, suggest that, yet again, for perfectly understandable human reasons, in manufacturers' minds *measurable* factors – cost and price – may have taken precedence over less measurable factors – quality and value. And that in this respect, they may have been out of sympathy with their customers for longer than *Design* magazine suggests.

There are important national and economic implications in all this. How, in the future, is Britain going to earn its living? Not, it would seem, from making heavy industrial goods and selling them to a captive imperial market. Not, it would seem, from making millions of very small things more cheaply than anyone else. And not, it would seem, from being a net exporter of natural resources.

This would seem to leave us with only one alternative: to recognise talent, to encourage talent, to reward talent. And to apply that talent to goods and services, hardware and software. In the real sense of that much-used phrase – to *add value*.

It is my hypothesis, open to challenge, dispute and debate, that this is precisely what the best of advertising does. A kind of talent is applied to commercial persuasion which makes both the persuasion *and* the subject of that persuasion more valuable. We shouldn't study advertising as though it were a minor art form. If it's to be justified, advertising has to be as functional as a fork-lift truck; and like the fork-lift truck, it must return more than its cost to the advertiser who invests in it.

What intrigues me are the skills and talents that can improve the return on that investment. They are immeasurable means to a measurable end, not an end in themselves. They are akin to the skills of advocates in other fields. The *length* of a counsel's speech for the defence can be easily established; yet it may not matter very much. What matters far more is that barrister's mastery of his/her subject, his understanding of the jury, the sequence of his argument, the balance of reason and emotion, his timing, his ability to use analogy and metaphor to evoke, to provoke – to persuade. None of us can measure those talents. I know only – and I suspect I'm not alone – that if I were charged with murder, I'd be a great deal more concerned about my advocate's talent than I would be about his price or the length of time he chose to speak.

Saving on the chardonnay: your very own conference theme while-u-wait

An edited version of a speech given at a Marketing Society pre-conference dinner, 1995. The annual Marketing Society conference is held in London in November and is preceded by a dinner on the night before in the Great Room of the Grosvenor House Hotel. The speaker is expected to say something relevant about marketing while keeping 1,200 marketing persons from going to sleep or throwing bread rolls.

It is my reluctant duty this evening to do two things.

First, according to my brief from the Society, I am to introduce and explain the conference theme to you. And second, I am to draw some lofty lessons from the past which might still be of value to us as we trundle off down the superhighway.

So that, dutifully, having made it quite clear to you that it wasn't my idea, is what I shall – at quite astonishing length – attempt to do.

I am bound to say that I find it a great deal easier to introduce the conference theme than to explain it to you. It has, as I'm sure you know, just three words: future; marketing; the. (Though not in that order.)

When I was first told about it, the conference committee had already gone firm on the words but was still apparently locked in dispute over the punctuation.

Was it to be: 'Marketing – The Future?'? Or without the question mark since the future could reasonably be expected to arrive? Or was it to be 'Marketing the Future'? (An ambitious project, certainly, but surely not beyond the combined talents of the Society.)

Conscious, perhaps, of some lingering ambiguity, the conference literature later added what was presumably meant to be an explanatory thought. It said: *'If you're not part of the future, you're part of the past.'*

I'll just pause here for moment so that you can take that in.

Right, now let me take you through it slowly. On second thoughts, why do I need to? Let me just call it profoundly simplistic, transparently opaque, self-evidently enigmatic. And so on.

I've always been fond of slogans that play about with time. One, which gives me great comfort even as I speak, is: Remember that tomorrow, today will be yesterday. I once invented an all-purpose slogan for an all-purpose corporate campaign for an all-purpose company. It said: Anglo-Galvanized (put your company name here): *Where Past and Future Meet.*

All corporate affairs directors love that slogan. The earnest ones love it because they say it sums up the very drive and spirit of their company and the bright ones love it because it's got something for both the retiring chairman and the new young chief executive – while on examination meaning absolutely nothing. Unlike, naturally, this year's conference theme.

If you're not part of the future, you're part of the past. So if you *are* part of the future, you aren't part of the past. Or rather, you weren't. And if you're only *part* of the past, what else were you doing?

I will, I promise – well, threaten, I suppose – return to the conference theme – all conference themes, as a matter of fact – in due course. But not until I've done my second duty – the lofty lesson from the past bit.

If you ask a lot of bright young graduates what they want to do with their lives, quite a lot of them these days say they want to go into marketing. Very gratifying – until you come to think about it. Thousands of very bright graduates out there, all wanting to do your jobs. (And *they* aren't part of the past, I can tell you.)

And then you ask them what exactly they'd like to market and they look confused. They've never thought about that. They just want to go into marketing; to market anything: personal pensions, package holidays, potato chips or charities. Because they've read that marketing is now a discrete and recognised skill in its own right and they want to practise it.

Then, have you noticed those little items in the trade press: barely rewritten press releases, most of them: 'Anglo-Galvanized announce the appointment of Clive Thrust as marketing manager, Aggregates. He has previously held similar positions with Scottish Widows, Pedigree Petfoods, Rentokil and the Bristol Zoo.'

Is there no limit to Clive's abilities? (I've always thought that almost everybody in marketing was called Clive. As a matter of interest, how many Clives are there here tonight?) [*A show of hands revealed a great many.*]

Now compare that fictional press release with another fictional press release.

'Anglo-Galvanized announce the appointment of Geoffrey Turner as production director, Aggregates. He has previously held similar positions with Häagen-Daaz, Vodafone, Mothercare and the Royal Bank of Scotland.'

You just wouldn't believe it about Geoff, would you? But you would about Clive. Production needs expert knowledge of the specific product. Marketing – apparently – doesn't.

It made a lot of sense, all those years ago, when marketing began to emerge as an identified skill. And it was also good news when people said that proper marketing was not just a skill, but a management process that should be the focal point for a company's total activity. (If you find these phrases a touch on the portentous side, it's because they've been lifted straight from your Society's literature.)

But then, I think, something else began to happen. Marketing is supposed to begin, metaphorically speaking, inside the factory and extend all the way to the final satisfied or dissastisfied user. But as marketing began to be more of a job than a process, its starting point began to move, very, very slowly and again very metaphorically, from inside the factory to outside the factory gates.

As the discrete skill of something called marketing has become more and more free-standing, more and more portable, more and more applicable to Scottish Widows, Pedigree Petfoods, Rentokil and the Bristol Zoo – so, unsurprisingly, it's become increasingly detached from design and production. As marketing persons go from pizzas to pension-schemes to OTC medicines, they've neither the time nor the inclination to learn much about the creation and manufacture of any of those items. They simply apply their all-purpose skills to selling more and more of what already exists.

All the best books on marketing tell us that this shouldn't be the case: that proper marketing starts with the wants and needs of the consuming public; that long before promotion begins, product design should match identified market.

But in real life, it doesn't always happen. In real life, marketing all too often begins outside the factory gates. All too often, marketing has come to mean getting rid of more of what you already make.

And while Colin Thrust goes from job to job and becomes the role model for thousands of ambitious graduates – God help them – who gets increasingly neglected?

The inventor, that's who: the product designer, the engineer, the thinker-up of things, the chemist, the brewer, the boffin. The people who are obsessed by the product itself; who willingly accept that the sizzle's important, but who get their personal kicks from trying to make an ever better steak. Or, as it might be, a better personal pension, a better ice-cream or a better inclusive holiday.

Car companies used to be run by people who loved cars. They knew how to make cars themselves and were always trying to make them better. Retail companies used to be run by people who loved shops, and a hundred and something years ago, George Safford Parker was nutty about fountain pens. As businesses got bigger and more complex, these obsessive, impractical, product-driven enthusiasts couldn't cope any longer. They had to be helped: by money-men and lawyers and marketing persons and advertisement agents. Now they've been helped so much, they hardly exist any more.

You may remember the story of one of our greatest ever national makers, Isambard Kingdom Brunel. He was so ashamed of his socially inferior trade that he decided to give his two sons a better start in life by sending them to Harrow – where they were able to learn several dead languages and were never heard of again.

From that moment on, the status of the maker in this country has been in steady decline. Engineers are men in dungarees. Inventors, at best, are like Sir Clive Sinclair, slightly batty figures from an early Ealing comedy. And the rise and rise of marketing persons, through no fault of theirs, has done nothing to help.

There's almost a case for saying that this country is already too good at marketing: at least in its partial sense. Skilful marketing can patch things up – just as floundering governments try to patch things up through what they like to call presentation.

Skilful marketing can disguise – at least for long enough to be dangerous – the absence of research and development and innovation and invention. The marketing leg is over-used and grows stronger. And so, as is the way with these things, the invention and production leg withers through lack of exercise.

Now a little more research. I've mentioned inventors and product designers and production directors and chemists and engineers and brewers and thinkers-up of things: all key people, as we must surely agree, in a proper marketing process. And since this is the Marketing Society – just how many here tonight, as a full-time job, do any of those things? [*Another show of hands; except that very few were raised.*]

It's all a bit like the old light bulb jokes, really. How many marketing men does it take?

I've always been intrigued by things called gift shops. 'Good morning sir, can I help you?' 'Thank you. It's my wife's birthday next week and I was thinking of giving her a parcel.' 'Well, you've certainly come to the right place, sir. Did you have anything particular in mind?' 'Yes – I rather thought something quite heavy but small enough to go in my briefcase.'

Gift shops exist to sell things to put into parcels – nobody much minds what. I would hate to see marketing going any further in that direction but I fear it might.

As the means of communication available to us become ever more distractingly fascinating, rightly and irresistibly so, there's a very real risk that we'll think even more about the how, and even less about the what; that the sizzle will continue to be valued more than the steak; that the parcel will become even more important than the object inside.

It might even be, I think, that the erosion of our manufacturing sector, and the rise and rise of our service sector, is in part connected with the decoupling of making things from marketing things.

So if this is a drift – and if it's a drift with unhelpful future consequences – who should we look to to correct it?

My own view is that we should look no further (and again I quote from the literature) than to *the* professional body for senior practising marketing people.

And that's my lofty lesson from the past, for the future. (And perhaps I should remind you at this point, that if you're not part of the past, you can't have had enough experience to be here tonight.)

And now, as I threatened, to the theme of your conference – Marketing the Future – or words to that effect.

Thinking up themes for conferences must be one of life's least rewarding occupations. Sales conferences are worst, though it'll be easy enough next year of course – it always is in Olympics year. They'll all be called *Going for Gold*. I've often thought that it would be somehow more British to call a conference *Settling for Silver*. I mean, I'd settle for silver, any time. Not at all bad, coming second. And a great deal more realistic. But I could never find a sales director to agree with me. Funny lot, sales directors.

Anyway, you all know how marketing conference themes are produced. First, the Society appoints a committee, then the full committee appoints a conference sub-committee. Then the conference sub-committee subpoenas five of its most inventive members to become the conference theme sub-sub-committee. And they meet. And they meet. Creatively drained, they open a bottle or two of chardonnay. And they meet again.

And after five months, they've cracked it. The breakthrough. Eureka! Marketing the Future. (Punctuation yet to be determined, but one thing at a time chaps.)

It's my pleasure this evening to tell you how it should be done.

Earlier this year, I commissioned some research into all the marketing conferences that have ever been held since marketing was invented and submitted their themes to rigorous linguistic analysis. A fascinating fact emerged. In the phrasing of the 3,412 themes analysed, a total of no more than 30 different words was used.

Words, for example, to pick a couple at random, such as Marketing and Future.

Now clearly, once this fact is known, planning becomes a great deal easier. We can, as we say in our business, eliminate the variables. Conference theme planning becomes a matter not of months, but of minutes. I now plan to demonstrate this with your help. As a gift from us all to your new director general, we shall shortly present him with next year's conference theme.

I have brought with me tonight five wooden cubes. On each side of each cube is written one of the 30 recognised marketing conference words. (Such as 'future' and 'marketing'.)

Please note that I call them cubes. It would be quite wrong to associate a discipline as rigorous as marketing with anything as irresponsible as dice. They are *cubes*; or to give them their full, registered descriptor, *Conference Planning Cubes*.

They are, you should know, the world's first Conference Planning Cubes.

Let me explain first the procedure and then the rules.

My independent assistant Melvyn Simpson, starting now, will hand one cube to each of the five tables in front of me.

I will then ask the first table to roll a cube and call out the word on the upward-facing surface; then the second – and so on.

Within one minute we will have five words.

Now here are the rules. Of the five words available, at least three must be used in the composition of next year's conference theme. No significant extra words may be added. Singulars may become plurals, and articles, prepositions, conjunctions and punctuation may be freely sprinkled, like salt and vinegar, at the customer's discretion. A re-roll is permissible under only two circumstances. First, if – as is only too likely – we end up with *this* year's theme. And second, if the result looks as if it's going to be deeply embarrassing for me.

These rules have been internationally recognised.

[*The five tables rolled the five dice and the following words were revealed in this order: Adding; Multinational; World; Dynamic; Future.*]

So, Nick – you'll be pleased to learn that your conference theme for next year will be: *The Future of Multinationals in a*

Dynamic World. Which makes a great deal more sense than…
well, many others, if you ask me.

All in two minutes. Not only democratic, but interactive.
And what a saving on the chardonnay.

Would you like us to do 1997 as well while we're about it?

These planning cubes will soon be on sale throughout the
developed world – and I'm in the process of designing other
sets for other purposes. There's to be one set for *political party*
conferences for example: where, interestingly, I've found a
need for only *two* cubes. And another set for executive titles in
advertisement agencies: strategic, deputy, managing, vice,
international, senior, worldwide, associate, president,
chairman, senior associate, global, multi-disciplinary – that
sort of thing. (Rather more cubes needed there.)

But before too long, there's one modification I'd like to
make to this original set.

Of the 30 words I found in my research, not one was
directly related to *making*. No invention, no production, no
product design. What I'd like to do – when the Marketing
Society has flexed its muscles and rehabilitated the great
makers and reintroduced making into marketing – is introduce
a sixth cube, with all those solid, unfashionable product and
manufacturing words on it. And then we can have another roll
and see what comes up.

George Safford Parker, he who was nutty about fountain
pens, once said: *'Make something better and people will buy it.'*

As a conference theme, it has much to be said for it: though
not nearly as much, naturally, as the theme for this year's
conference; which, as instructed, I shall now explain to you.

Tomorrow's conference will concern itself with the future of
marketing.

I hope that's cleared things up.

I was going to wish you all a useful and inspiring
conference: but I understand that some of you, at least, *do*

think it's possible to be part of this evening without being part of tomorrow.

I suppose you know what you're doing. You can hardly claim you weren't warned. Just watch out for those graduates, that's all.

It now gives me great pleasure to ask Melvyn to present the world's first complete set of Marketing Conference Planning Cubes to your new director-general, Nick Turnbull – and through him, in perpetuity, to the Marketing Society; to thank you for your attention; and to hope that – most of you at least – will find some sort of future to be a part of.

Never use irony in Chicago

Prompted first by Marshall McLuhan and later infamously championed by Theodore Levitt, globalism (terrible word) started to get the marketing and advertising worlds over-excited in the mid-seventies. In its more extreme interpretations, global marketing was alleged to mean that you could now sell the same products in the same way all over the world. Levitt once claimed that the needs and wants of the world's consumers had become 'irrevocably homogenized'. It was always absolutely apparent that this was not the case but people in marketing – particularly people in multinational companies – are curiously afraid to challenge new wisdoms. To question globalism was to run the risk of seeming out-of-touch and parochial. Besides, most large companies were attempting to expand internationally and to have global ambitions made them feel good. The nearest the world has yet come to a truly global product is probably Coca-Cola which to this day is beyond the reach of more than half the world's population. Though globalism is now to a large extent discredited, the word 'global' continues to be freely used. It should be interpreted as meaning 'in as many as two other countries apart from its country of origin'. The following piece appeared in *Commercials* 13 years after the events it described, to coincide with the 1989 Screen Advertising Film Festival in Cannes.

It was in 1976 that Chicago first discovered the rest of the world. Every year, *Advertising Age* organises its well-attended Advertising Workshop and in 1976 it decided to devote it to the sexy new phenomenon of global communications.

The people from *Advertising Age* got in touch with J. Walter Thompson in New York – just who they talked to I never discovered, but I'd still like to know – and asked if the agency would take part. All they wanted was a three-hour presentation with examples of international advertising in all media, from all over the world, accompanied by definitive views and conclusions.

J. Walter Thompson New York, anxious as ever to oblige an influential trade paper, said of course, only too pleased, no problem, thank you for thinking of us.

There was then a gap of some weeks while J. Walter Thompson NY glowed in the gratitude that had beamed their way from Chicago. *Advertising Age* then wrote asking for details of the presentation: title, names of the participants and so on. They were, they explained, finalising their first mailing shot. For the first time, J. Walter Thompson NY realised that, in agreeing to undertake the presentation, they had not actually completed their obligation.

It's a well-established fact that the word 'international' is a synonym for foreign. What *Advertising Age* wanted, therefore, was a presentation about foreign advertising. It followed that it would be quite wrong (so went the reasoning) for J. Walter Thompson US to undertake the task of putting together a three-hour presentation of foreign advertising in all media within two months. Quite improper. But they had, they remembered handily, some foreign branches.

It was then that I got the telephone call to say that my name had been enthusiastically accepted by the *Advertising Age* organisers as the team leader and would I please let them (J. Walter Thompson US) know if there was anything at all they could do to help, such as make hotel reservations? In the meantime, good luck and goodbye.

When I got the mailer from *Advertising Age*, it spoke excitedly about the new tidal wave of globalism. It told me that ideas were now crossing national frontiers with the speed of jet planes and that the needs and wants of the world's citizens were now irrevocably homogenised and a lot more stuff along similar lines.

The mailer then went on to say that the J. Walter Thompson presentation would illustrate the truth of all this, which I noted with interest since I'd never been sold on its existence let alone its value.

Having had the project so deftly delegated to me, it was clear that I needed to do a bit of the same. So I recruited my J. Walter Thompson equivalents from four other cities: George from Frankfurt, Bob from Toronto, Tony from Sydney and (confusingly) Hans from Sao Paulo. In itself, this was a good idea. What I suggested we did, however, was not.

Whenever I had visited other J. Walter Thompson offices around the world and been shown their work, I had been struck by one recurring comment. Whoever was introducing the work would say: 'Now this next one's probably not going to mean a great deal to you because you won't know that our most popular national leisure activity is earwig racing and this commercial uses the language of earwig racing to imply that only Bard's beer makes you virile though of course in this country you aren't allowed actually to show the beer which is why we use this famous comedian who you won't recognise because unfortunately he's unknown outside this country but the catchphrase he uses is as good as saying Bard's to most people because of a sponsorship programme he did for them five years ago. Anyway, see what you think. It's been amazingly successful and since it started sales have gone up by nearly 26 per cent ...'.

And sure enough, I'd look at the commercial and it wouldn't mean anything to me at all. But I did believe the sales figures so I had to believe that what I'd just looked at was a piece of successful advertising.

I also believed them because whenever, in turn, I was showing the London reel to visitors I would find myself saying, 'Now this next one's probably not going to mean a great deal to you ...'. (Have you ever tried to explain the nature and appeal of mushy peas to a Californian?)

Convinced, therefore, that much of the world's most original and effective advertising was quite incomprehensible except to those to whom it was addressed, I encouraged George, Bob, Tony and Hans to bring with them as many examples of obscure and effective national advertising as they could find. At the same time, I asked them to bring examples of equally effective work that they believed could be understood just about anywhere.

We all pitched up at the Conrad Hilton in Chicago. The Conrad Hilton in Chicago is the world's friendliest hotel. I know this because it says so outside in 30-foot-high neon lettering.

There were just four days to go before the presentation and we had nothing written down. We had several hundred commercials, but no idea which we were going to use, let alone in what order – so they were all still on their separate 16mm spools. We worked in a large room which had been set up by an immensely helpful crew from J. Walter Thompson Chicago as editing suite, viewing room, typing pool and fast-food joint.

Each of us started by showing the others the work we'd brought with us, and at almost every turn we found ourselves saying, 'Now this next one probably won't mean a great deal to you, but in my country …'.

We then assembled the best of these into an obscure/national reel and started to write a linking commentary. This consisted mostly of finding different ways of saying, 'Now this next one probably won't … but in Germany/Japan/Yorkshire/New South Wales it's long been a tradition that …'.

We then assembled the commercials which, we all agreed, *did* communicate readily to all of us, with little or no explanatory introduction. Hardly surprisingly, we discovered that they all set out to appeal to what we chose to call global tribes – a word we came to prefer to target groups.

An advertiser offering beauty to women, or rebellion to teenagers, or masculinity to smokers, or luxury to business travellers, could successfully use common stimuli to evoke universal responses: as long, of course, as those stimuli were universally and consistently recognised.

We were reminded that many of the (relatively few) global campaigns owed much of their universality to the common denominator of the movies. Very few people, even Americans, had ever seen a real cowboy: Marlboro's campaign could never have travelled if the Western hadn't been there first.

So we divided our presentation into an examination of different tribes. We found tribes which contained members from all countries, and tribes which contained members from only one country. We also found tribes which contained members from only one region.

And we found, hardly surprisingly, that the advertising that worked best was that which understood those tribes best.

I then wrote the introduction. Into eight minutes, I packed every cliché I could retrieve about the new globalism. I raided McCluhan and Levitt and *Advertising Age* itself.

I talked about the world getting smaller and ideas crossing frontiers with the speed of jet planes, and the aspirations of the housewife in Nicaragua being identical to those of her counterparts in the Netherlands and the electronic village and new universalisms of communications.

And to demonstrate the validity of what I was saying, I showed a very recent commercial from Great Britain. In Welsh.

This idea was not too clever by half. It was not clever at all. Nobody understood it. Irony is a dangerous game at the best of times. On a hot August day in Chicago, I'm now in a position to tell you, it is terminal.

As I discovered later, it was at this point that one of the journalists left the room, never to return. He later wrote an appreciative report of the full three hours which was headlined: 'World Growing Smaller Says JWT Staffer.'

Do not believe the old saying that good advertising speaks for itself. Good advertising speaks for itself only to those for whom it is intended. Much good advertising speaks quite deliberately in code, or uses a secret language, and excludes the rest of us. That's one of the reasons why it's good.

Being exposed to things you don't understand is very bad for the self-esteem. For many hours, we showed that Chicago audience things they didn't understand, having told them beforehand that they weren't going to understand them, and then explaining to them afterwards why they hadn't. They didn't warm to us.

About the only piece of work they did understand was the Australian commercial which showed a dog called Kevin peeing on the wheel of a Leyland truck.

The radio version went: 'Kevin may have done it on a Leyland truck but Kevin never done it on me.' When I say they understood it, I suppose I mean that they understood *what* was happening rather than *why* it was happening. I don't think any of us understood that.

Around this time of the year, international juries drawn from the outstanding advertising talent of all nations gather in darkened screening rooms to pass judgment on thousands of other people's commercials.

There's nobody there to say to them: 'Now this next one probably won't mean much to you but in my country ...'. Sometimes there's a synopsis: 'In this scenario the goblin robs the children of their porridge. A light-hearted tune punches home the sales message.' Synopses are not always of great value.

How can these juries, however well-intentioned, understand commercials that were cunningly devised to be generally incomprehensible? Of course they can't – and sensible national agencies won't have entered them.

If they are wise, they will enter just that work which genuinely does speak for itself – to everyone. You've only got to sit in the Cannes cinema on the final night to know that such work exists. Within a split second of the end of a commercial, there's a sharp crack of applause from absolutely everybody present – irrespective of age or nationality.

Something has worked for all of them, instantly – and that something, of course, is a universal something. All round the world, dogs pee on truck wheels. All round the world, children fart in baths. It is far more often visual demonstration than verbal assertion.

The commercials that are recognised by international juries almost by definition deserve to be: they've proved that they can communicate immediately with many different people from many different countries. What an international jury can never be expected to do is recognise a piece of work it doesn't understand – particularly one that hasn't been entered in the first place.

As the global gospellers begin to sound ever less persuasive, it is the coded tribal messages we should increasingly look at with respect.

2
What advertising does

Why reality in advertising is to be avoided at all costs

Marketing, November 1996

Of all the time-honoured accusations levelled at advertising, its refusal to reflect a true picture of the real world is one of the most familiar. It is, we are told, a failure to face up to reality.

In fact, of course, advertising is absolutely right to avoid featuring the real world. Advertising's most common function is to bring out the best in things, to make its subjects as attractive as possible. The real world is full of dirty finger nails, derelict housing estates and dog turds. These are unwelcome associations for personal equity plans and freeze-dried coffee granules.

Advertising people should not see themselves as courageous chroniclers of gritty, social truths. Rather, they should model themselves on costermongers, cosmeticians, auctioneers, wedding photographers and taxidermists.

Apples look better when polished up a little. The lumpen husband will think it money well spent if the boil on his neck is away from camera and he comes out looking like Hugh Grant. An auctioneer who adopted the Roy Brooks school of advocacy ('this hideous painting is almost certainly a fake and would be over-priced at a guinea') might soon have to take his children out of private school. And who, in the interests of truth and documentary realism, wants their old, dead poodle to come back from the taxidermist looking like an old, dead poodle?

There is an innocent and valued role in life for those of us who try to help things look their best. We should not allow ourselves to be bullied into feeling guilty about it.

We are most commonly mocked, of course, for our portrayal of families. There have never been families, our critics say, like the families we put in advertisements: daddy and mummy, he in jacket and tie, she in her pinny, sitting around the breakfast table with one small girl and one rather bigger boy, sunshine streaming through the window and milk decanted from the Tetra-Pak into a blue-and-white striped jug.

What a travesty, what a parody, what a lie!

This month, as you must have noticed, research has once again revealed that the cause of our continued national decline is the disappearance of the British nuclear family and with it the structured meal.

But did you also notice the photographs that accompanied these stories?

They were all captioned 'The Family – as it used to be' and they showed daddy and mummy, he in jacket and tie, she in her pinny, sitting around the breakfast table with one small girl and one rather bigger boy, sunshine streaming through the window – and milk decanted from the Tetra-Pak into a blue-and-white striped jug.

Look even more closely, and you could find a smaller caption: *Photo: Advertising Archives.*

So it seems that the cause of our continued national decline is the fact that we no longer have families of the kind that everybody knows we never had in the first place. A bit of a failure to face up to reality, if you ask me.

Cheese rind and chicken shit – that's progress for you

Marketing, October 1995

Once upon a time, all cheddar cheese came with its rind on. Since you bought by weight and the rind was inedible, you incurred both cost and inconvenience.

Time passes. Market forces work. Consumer dissatisfaction is identified and a new, improved cheddar is made available: new, *rindless* cheddar. With waste eliminated and convenience enhanced, you are, reasonably enough, invited to pay a little more for it. Rindless cheddar represents progress.

So far, no problem. Rational man nods approvingly. Time passes.

Market forces move again. New dissatisfactions are identified. And a new, improved cheddar is made available: new, mature cheddar *with rind*. Both waste and inconvenience have been restored; but you are, nevertheless, invited to pay a little more for it. Farmhouse cheddar *with rind* represents progress.

Rational man's brow furrows. Hang on a minute. If cheese with its rind on used to be cheaper than cheese with its rind off, why is cheese with its rind off now cheaper than cheese with its rind on? How can it be progress to go from A to B and also from B to A? Unless going from A to B in the first place was a mistake in which case it wasn't progress. What's going on here?

Rational man may reach for one of two explanations.

First, that the cheese rind scandal is but an infinitesimal part of The Great Marketing Conspiracy. Vance Packard first exposed it over 40 years ago. Brilliant young men and women, many of them university graduates, first create and then exploit rampant consumer insecurity.

Virtual dissatisfactions are identified, promoted and then gratified by virtual product improvements. All change justifies higher price. Progress doesn't necessarily require forward movement; movement in any direction will do nicely, thank you. Bond salesmen call it churning.

And the second, much less interesting, explanation is this. Good marketing has no place for dogma or intolerance. Rind on cheese means different things to different people. People who like it off are right to want it off. People who like it on are right to want it on. And the people who make and market cheese are right to make and market both.

So the cheese rind story is not scandal but parable. It explains why all monopolies are suspect and why centralism is doomed to fail the individual. And that's the explanation I prefer.

Once upon a time, eggs were sold loose, their shells often bearing unmistakable signs of their farmyard origins. Time passed, market forces worked, consumer dissatisfaction was identified and quite soon eggs came hosed down, scrubbed up, spotlessly sanitised. Clean eggs represented progress, and people were happy to pay for it.

But of course those university graduates were never going to be satisfied for long. So today, you can buy free-range eggs with a tiny, curly hen's feather in every box. It can't be long before we're offered, for very little extra, free-range eggs *now with genuine chicken shit.*

I don't expect to buy them but I'll be pleased to know I could.

If you make 'em laugh, do you make 'em buy?

In the 1970s, when I wrote this, there was more 'humorous' advertising in the US than there was in the UK – or so it seemed. During the 1980s, the position was reversed. In the early 1990s, as the recession hit advertising expenditure, there were those who blamed advertisers' inconstancy at least in part on the 1980s agencies' obsession with entertainment at, allegedly, the expense of effectiveness. The advertising business, so the argument went, by failing to fulfil its primary function of selling, had so devalued its own product that its clients deserted as soon as times got difficult. At the same time, there was new evidence that 'likeability' in advertising was a near-constant factor in successful campaigns. While people continue to discuss the question in general terms – as if it's all good or all bad for all tasks at all times – I expect we shall continue to see examples of extreme turgidity, examples of extreme facetiousness and quite a lot of reasonable stuff in the middle. In the UK, in the late 90s, in television advertising particularly, there is still much work that sets out to entertain: but more often than not now, in relevant product categories.

The question, 'Does humour sell?' belongs to that fine family of advertising questions none of which is likely to be answered definitively but all of which will continue indefinitely to be asked. Other favourites include: 'What is the optimum level of advertising expenditure?', 'How many times should a commercial be shown?', 'Is a 30-second commercial better than a half-page in the *Daily Mirror*?' and 'What about nudity, then?'

It is, however, both sensible and respectable to persist in asking these questions, so long as both questioner and questioned resist the temptation to establish or accept glib and all-embracing dogma.

With luck, and hedged about by inevitable questions such as 'What is humour?' and 'What is advertising?', it should be possible to begin to say how, in certain circumstances, certain kinds of humour may fruitfully be used in the advertising of certain products – at least for the time being. If anybody thinks that too inconclusive, hypothetical and unsatisfactory an objective, he should perhaps choose to earn his living in some simpler and more measurable occupation.

Humour can be kind or cruel; broad or subtle; largely visual or totally dependent on a collision of words. It can be trivial and facetious, or deadly serious in its undertones. Between the poles of satire and slapstick lie an almost infinite number of levels and variations of humour. And as with every kind of communication, each form of humour will be understood and enjoyed only if the listener (or looker) is capable of making that final and necessary act of completion.

A joke which nobody sees is not a joke. A joke which one person in a hundred sees is not a joke to the other 99. If the concept of irony is alien to the receiver, he may accept the irony at face-value, and so not only miss the point, but interpret the message in a way diametrically opposite from the way the sender of that message had intended. (It would be interesting to know, for example, what proportion of the loyal viewers of *Till Death Us Do Part* accepted Alf Garnett as the long-awaited spokesman for all that was right and shrewd and sensible. And equally interesting to speculate just how much bigger that proportion might have been in the absence of studio laughter.)

Humour, then, has no universal and objective values. It will always be judged individually and subjectively. A man in a top hat slipping on a banana skin may strike almost everybody as fairly funny; but even that primitive incident relies for its humour on some prior knowledge, some prior attitudes, and some ability to contribute on the part of its observers.

Unless the top hat is known to symbolise the upper classes, unless the observer is already against the upper classes, and unless the observer is capable, however subconsciously, of seeing the undignified upending of a single figure as a comment on the fallibility of privilege, then not only will the incident fail to amuse but indeed it is likely to arouse sympathy and concern. (Few people are likely to be amused by the sight of a frail old lady slipping on a banana skin; but it's just possible that her best friend, slightly older but for years made to feel inferior, might.)

However, there is one characteristic which all forms of humour seem to share (and indeed without which they would fail to be humorous) and that is their *ability to reveal.* Humour, when it works, makes people think; it makes them see the familiar from an unfamiliar point of view. And it makes people think not only painlessly but pleasurably.

This pleasure comes not just from the revelation itself, but from the self-congratulation that derives from a contribution made. Just as a joke will fail if it asks too much of a recipient, so it will fail if it asks nothing. If the point is explained, the recipient is denied the chance to participate: and there's no flash-moment of perception and pleasure.

So all humour, however broad and however universally understood, is implicit rather than explicit: an explicit joke is either not explicit or not a joke.

All good comedians, all good storytellers, all good makers of advertisements, entice their receivers into willing and constructive collaboration. It's a skilful, delicate and difficult thing to do – particularly in advertising where the pressures of committees and cost tend to favour the 'explicit', the 'unambiguous', the 'message which just can't fail to be understood'.

But the measure of a good joke is much the same as the measure of a good advertisement (judging it now purely in terms of its communications effectiveness). Has it asked enough, but not too much, of its selected audience? Has it allowed that audience to see something for itself? (Whether, in the case of the advertisement, what the audience comes to see is the most persuasive and relevant thing is clearly another question.)

So the principles of humour and the principles of commercial persuasion are very close. Many years ago, the Ford Motor Company wanted to tell American motorists that they sold more convertibles than did any other automobile manufacturer. They could perfectly well have said: 'America's bestselling convertible.' Instead they ran a headline which read: 'The only convertible that outsells Ford.' And the picture was of a baby-carriage.

That is a kind of humour; and it's almost a joke. It certainly depends entirely on a contribution from its audience for the communication to be complete. But the contribution is a small and pleasurable one, well within the capacity of anyone in the market for a car. And what could have been a piece of self-congratulatory manufacturer's so-whattery became engaging evidence of confident leadership. The point had been seen.

In the pursuit of better advertisements, there is probably more to be learned from a study of the anatomy of humour than from any other subject.

When we come to look at the deliberate use of humour in advertising, it is as well to remember this basic similarity of principle. Advertising humour becomes discredited largely because of its misuse, mainly in connection with two great advertising misconceptions:

1. Television is an entertainment medium, therefore commercials must entertain.
Not true, of course: first, television is not an entertainment medium. It's a medium, just as the telephone system is a medium, and twice as versatile. It is no more an entertainment medium than news print is a news medium. It can be used to educate, to carry news, to tell stories.

Second: even if a high proportion of television time is devoted to what sets out to be entertainment, it clearly does not follow that all commercials for all products addressed to all people should also seek to divert. Involve, yes; reward, ideally; entertain, not necessarily.

2. This is a low-interest product. Unless we do something funny, they'll go and put the kettle on.
Any product good enough to be bought, and bought again, is of interest to the people who buy it. (It may, however, be of low interest to the creative people, in which case they should be trained or fired.)

This attitude leads to blind headlines ('Let's intrigue them so they just have to read the copy'), mindless use of borrowed interest ('Why don't we get Mick Jagger?'), and animated spokesmen with funny voices mouthing otherwise conventional copy-points. Such advertising may not bore, but neither will it persuade.

One of the most important and difficult functions of advertising is to show the familiar and the relatively mundane in a new light. Anyone in advertising who backs away from this inconvenient fact and relies instead on irrelevant and dissociated excitement is abdicating from one of his more important responsibilities.

If humour is to be used relevantly and effectively, a distinction should first be made between products bought from housekeeping money and those from pocket money. Most women buying most products from a limited housekeeping budget like to feel they've bought prudently and well. For them, shopping is part of their profession; possibly enjoyable, sometimes sociable, but serious.

There are certain kinds of humour – the clever-clever, the superficial, the transient, the slick, the over-sophisticated – that will, simply through association, begin to make the products themselves seem superficial and cheap. A repeat purchase product, bought out of housekeeping money, runs a considerable risk of losing its reputation for substance and quality if it's consistently promoted in a jokey manner.

This is still more true of proprietary medicines, even those bought for relatively trivial complaints. There can be a kind of seesaw in people's minds: when the fun end goes up, the effectiveness end goes down. That long-running series of highly entertaining commercials for Alka Seltzer in the States, having successfully jolted the product into the twentieth century, must surely, sooner or later, run the risk of sapping the product of its medicinal magic. And when the magic goes, so will the effectiveness of the product.

But there's another kind of humour which, significantly, we tend to call good humour. Far from being superficial, it can manifest a deep understanding of, and affection for, humanity. People are seen to be real people, with frailties and fallibilities and vanities and perversities. This kind of humour has practically universal appeal. It has permanence and substance and warmth. It reaches the heart as well as the head; evokes a smile rather than a laugh. This kind of humour is perfectly in keeping with the nature and function of everyday, housekeeping products.

Some products, though, are bought not from housekeeping money but from pocket money. The purchasers are more likely to be men than women – presumably because women aren't so easily able to give themselves pocket money. And pocket-money spending is an altogether different affair: freer, less regular, less responsible, more impulsive, more fun.

Schweppes, presumably, is a pocket-money product – bought if not by, then at least at the behest of, men. (Perhaps true in 1971, but clearly not in 1991.) And the style and the wit with which Schweppes presents itself to the public again seems true to the nature of the product and the circumstances of its consumption. Humour here, far from debasing the value of the product, is enhancing it; is giving it an extrinsic value that must make life very difficult for its competitors.

If you examine very closely all those very funny American commercials we view with such envy and respect, you'll find that a very high proportion of them are for products bought by or for men, from pocket money. Alternatively, they are for products aimed at a small minority of people. It is tempting, but ill-advised, to try to apply a style of wit and humour that is right and relevant for a pocket-money, minority-audience product to a mass-consumption, housekeeping-money product.

Much more could be written; but perhaps the main points to summarise are these:

1. The principles of humour and the principles of making good advertisements are similar: both should 'reveal'.

2. Communication is most successful when the recipient makes the final contribution himself. Creative skill is needed to ensure that the recipient cannot fail to arrive at the desired conclusion.

3. Economy is not just brevity but implicitness. And for the recipient to contribute, a degree of implicitness is essential.

4. Humour will always be assessed individually and subjectively. What is funny to you may be incomprehensible to your target audience: and they are the only ones who matter.

5. Humour, when used, should spring naturally from the product, or from the need the product is there to satisfy.

6. Consistent use of irrelevant and superficial humour can call into question the intrinsic worth and quality of a product.

7. Good humour can be affectionate and kind, and can be evidence of a human and understanding advertiser.

8. Expensive products are not necessarily serious, nor cheap ones frivolous. It's more important to consider the kind of money with which they are bought: does it come from a restricted weekly housekeeping budget or from discretionary pocket money?

9. Wit, irony, understatement and allusion may be understood and appreciated by a minority of people. For products designed for those people, such humour can add appreciably to their extrinsic value.

10. The nature of the humour used must always be true to the nature of the product (or its desired nature) and to the nature of its present and potential users.

One of many batty old observations about marketing

Marketing, March 1997

This is the first in an occasional series about batty sayings which have gone too long unchallenged, thus denying marketing persons many zillions of units of currency and inflicting upon them almost as many deeply tiresome dinner-party conversations.

This is what Ralph Waldo Emerson (1803–1882) is famously believed to have said: 'If a man write a better book, preach a better sermon, or make a better mouse-trap than his neighbour, tho' he build his house in the woods, the world will make a beaten path to his door.'

To the financial director and the dinner-party didact, these are thrilling words. So who needs marketing? Who needs advertising?

I'll tell you who: that sanctimonious, pen-pushing mouse-murderer, that's who. And if you don't believe me, try this simple experiment.

Go into deep woods and build yourself a new house. As soon as it is completed, first write and then deliver a better sermon. Then wait.

The following day make a better mouse-trap. And wait again.

Only if you are still unconvinced should you bother to write a better book.

Because I am sorry to have to tell you that there will be no beaten path. Rather, such path as there was will soon be overgrown from disuse.

We know five things about Emerson's man. He writes books; he preaches sermons; he builds mouse-traps; and –

despite living in the middle of a wood – he has a neighbour. (Eerily, this neighbour has precisely the same eclectic set of hobbies but apparently pursues them with less skill.) We also know that however great the books, the sermons and the mouse-traps may be – and however much the world would appreciate them were the world to know of their existence – he is doomed to disappointment for as long as global ignorance persists.

The mouse-trap saying is a killer on two counts. For those who have no time for marketing, it provides glib and authoritative support. And for those who have too much faith in marketing, it is so transparently silly that it even deters them from the wholly admirable pursuit of better mouse-traps. Almost on its own, this potty apothegm has bred the belief that, since good products sell themselves, only bad products need marketing.

Among those who believe that the intelligent Emerson never uttered these words may be counted myself and Elbert Hubbard. There is absolutely no written record of Emerson ever having used them: and the only attribution occurs in a book published seven years after his death in which a lady claims to have heard him say them.

Elbert Hubbard, insanely in my view, vigorously contested this suggestion, claiming authorship for himself – much to the posthumous relief, I would imagine, of Ralph Waldo Emerson.

And, no: I don't know who Elbert Hubbard was, either.

Elastic brands

Written for *Marketing Week* in 1988. As the cost and risk of launching orphan brands continue to increase (see *What sort of family does this Jaffa cake come from?* page 86), so does the attraction of stretching the authority of existing brands. Since the piece appeared, Prudential has retreated from estate agency and Wilkinson is into skin-care. The article prompted a telephone call from the secretary of the managing director of Jockey Ltd who wanted to know what size underpants I wore. It turned out that Y-Front is one of their registered trade marks and not available at Marks & Spencers. I'm happy to make this clear.

'There is also the possibility that M&S, which has had shaky success in North America so far, will nudge its own products into Brooks Brothers stores.' (*The Times*, 3/5/88)

'Good morning, sir. May I help you ?'

'Thank you. I would like one button-down cotton Oxford, size 15–33, in the solid blue; one pair of cordavan loafers, size 8E; and two cod-and-prawn fishcakes suitable for the microwave.'

'With pleasure, sir. Charge or cash?'

Just how far a brand reputation can be stretched without diluting the value of the original is one of the constantly fascinating debates in marketing. Cadbury's must have thought hard before it gave its name to milk powder; and even harder before going into instant mashed potato. Mars is surely right to use Pedigree for its petfoods. I haven't yet got used to Prudential as an estate agent, though that may be the fault of the boss-eyed cherokee.

Dunhill was clever to recognise that a reputation for classy cigarettes and lighters could be extended beyond smoking into classiness generally. It was a lot more logical to go from tobacco to tailoring than it would have been to launch a Dunhill roll-your-own.

Retailers' names have much greater elasticity than those of manufacturers: presumably because their skill is known to lie in selection rather than in making. Wilkinson Sword could go from secateurs to razor blades to (just) shaving cream. But not, I think, to aftershave to eau de toilette to challenging Poison. Harrods could, and do, stock the lot – and so could Boots.

Many people are so acutely conscious of the risks involved in attempts to (as we say in marketing) optimise a brand franchise, that timidity sets in. Parker Pen, at least in this country, agonised for some years before deciding to market a ballpoint; and even then it was called not a ballpoint but a ballpen to distinguish it (a subtlety lost on the public) from the Bics and the Biros. Parker's hesitation was prudent. All ballpoints at the time were cheap, plastic and disposable, and Parker was selling not writing instruments but expensive and lasting gifts. Until recently, cheques signed with anything other than a fountain pen had been invalid. In the event, it was in part the authority of the Parker name that brought respectability to the entire category.

The best way I know to test such timidity is to play a game christened, if not invented, by Doug Richardson. It's called Brandicide and its rules are so self-evident that I'll explain them to you.

Take any powerful brand – and mentally extend its name to a new venture of such a kind that the parent's brand values are not just diluted but killed outright. It's not as easy as it seems. After Eight Chewing Gum seemed a likely starter, but on reflection it seemed that the Parker effect might come into play and legitimise the sector: an adult, sophisticated chewing gum is not an impossibility. But After Eight *Bubble Gum* is another matter. Brandicide has been committed.

For an instant, the paragraph from the *Times* (above) conjured up the vision of a double death: two duellists killing one another simultaneously. Mariner's Bake and Madison Avenue: the immediate extinction of both Brooks Brothers and St. Michael. But I expect all they had in mind was Y-Fronts.

That toothpaste is an imposter!
(But who cares?)

Marketing, September 1995

There's a poster up at the moment featuring an outline toothpaste tube, a question mark, and the words: 'We're too busy improving our own to make it for anyone else.' It's signed off by Colgate.

National brand manufacturers who choose not to supply own label feel themselves a lot more virtuous than those who do, and get much aggrieved when their virtue goes unrewarded. They long to out their competitors by name but never do. Instead, whenever frustration becomes uncontainable, they instruct their agency to come up with an advertising campaign to trumpet their own purity while strongly implying the duplicity of others.

Understandable, certainly: but it's hard to believe that people will dutifully respond: 'Now that I know that Colgate do not manufacture toothpaste for others to sell under their own names, I shall from henceforth use no other.'

I've always suspected that paranoia over this issue springs from the widespread folly of believing respondents.

Get consumers into a focus group and ask them why they buy cheaper, retailer brands and they grope around, not unnaturally, for some self-enhancing justification. Or to put it another way, they lie. 'Well, they're all the same really, aren't they? I mean, everybody knows that. I mean, they're all made by Heinz/Nestlé/Kellogg's/Cadburys, aren't they? When you buy the brands, you're just paying for the adverts.'

And marketing directors study the transcripts and believe them and decide that it's time to be proactive and set the record straight through advertising.

The challenge to the agency is to find an angle. In this case, the angle is that Colgate is too busy improving its own toothpaste to make it for others: and I have to say that I do not find it persuasive. Too busy? All day, every day, improving? A toothpaste? You have a simple choice: to disbelieve it; or conclude that there's more room for improvement than an established brand should wish to boast about.

These nervous little campaigns may make manufacturers feel better, but I can't remember one that's rung true. The basic flaw, of course, is that if people like the retailer brands enough to go on buying them – and they're cheaper – why should they care who makes them?

The real value of national advertising is as it's always been – to establish and maintain for national brands an unargued air of confidence, superiority and worth. To start getting peevish, and in front of the punters at that, simply diminishes the brand's stature.

Heinz withdraws national television support from its brands. A couple of years later, it starts making baked beans for its retailing competitors. Maybe the two decisions were unconnected but the theory of brands suggests otherwise.

Big brands should remain, at least in public, pretty lofty: which is why comparative advertising is nearly always unwise for a brand leader.

There may well be a case for making known the fact that Colgate does't make toothpaste for anybody else. But why not through public relations or perhaps on pack?

Don't forget the absence factor: or why FMCGs become SMCGs

Marketing, August 1996

The problem facing a great many Fast-Moving Consumer Goods companies is that their goods move far too slowly. FMCGs get a lot of attention – but there's at least as much to learn from a study of SMCGs. They deserve a lot more recognition and perhaps even their own awards evening. My own nomination for the Grand Prix would probably go to Angostura Bitters.

SMCGs are usually slow-moving not because each unit takes an age to exhaust, but because consumers leave very long gaps between finishing one unit and starting another. If this is a symptom from which your own brand suffers, you may confidently diagnose it to be suffering from what we doctors call a low absence factor.

Some commodities have very high absence factors: petrol, for example; or loo paper; or cigarettes. You can't not know you haven't got them. But not all commodities, and even fewer brands, make their absence so tellingly felt. And the longer people manage without them, of course, the fainter the feeling of absence becomes until – the ultimate failure – you've got another lapsed user on your hands.

All ambitious brands should aim for a high absence factor but surprisingly few seem to do so. One of the most effective techniques has always been to couple your brand to a specific occasion. Only one kind of jam, for example, enjoys a high absence factor – and that's the one that's made from oranges and belongs to breakfast. Consumers invented bedtime drinks for themselves. Lemon Jif makes annual use of Shrove

Tuesday. Turkeys may not vote for Christmas but their breeders certainly would.

But then, all too often, greed sets in. 'You know, Nigel, we're crucifying this brand by limiting its appeal to bedtime. If we re-positioned it as the Anytime Drink, we could up consumption potential by a factor of four.' This is not just greedy, it's ignorant. By disconnecting the brand from bedtime, there will now be no daily prompt, no regular reminder, no automatic trigger. The Bedtime Drink becomes the Anytime Drink – and within a very few years the No-time Drink. Unnoticed and unmourned, its absence factor at zero, it disappears forever from the nation's shelves.

Another good wheeze is to look for a permanent visual reminder of an object's absence. This sounds difficult until you remember kitchen towels. There sits the empty holder on the kitchen wall, day after day, radiating reproach, until the consumer cracks. I'd love to know how the consumption of paper towels differed between households with holders and those without.

Trying to calculate how much things are missed can be a more helpful way of assessing brand strength than how much they are appreciated. If your brand's absence factor feels low, think kitchen towels, turkeys, cream eggs and marmalade.

Would Odorono smell as sweet by any other name?

Marketing, November 1996

Madonna is calling her daughter Lourdes. Perhaps she hopes that, as a result, her daughter will command respectful attention throughout her life. If so, she'll be disappointed. In common with a lot of other people, Madonna seems to be ignoring the unequivocal lessons of Odorono and the Earls Court Road.

New brand names come in two broad categories: full names and empty names.

Full names are favoured because they come furnished with ready-made relevant connotations: either descriptive or emotive. Ready-Brek, Band-Aid, Oven Pad and I Can't Believe It's Not Butter are all descriptive; Phileas Fogg, Fisherman's Friend, Golden Churn and Legendary Harley Davidson are emotive. So is Lourdes.

Empty names are favoured because they are sterilised and virus-free. Since they come with no baggage, they carry no undesirable overtones and can also be more easily registered in today's obligatory 293 countries. Ariel, Andrex, Kodak, Zantac were all, once, empty names. (They may have explicable origins, like Tesco and Amstrad, but no instant significance.) Numerals as names are just about as empty as you can get.

But once a brand is established, these pre-natal distinctions very rapidly disappear. Empty names, for good or ill, begin to fill up. They absorb the brand's values and begin to represent them. And full names show an even more disturbing tendency. Much to their godparents' dismay, the original carefully chosen, rigorously researched emotional associations are ruthlessly replaced with associations the brand actually deserves. They are rarely the same.

One of the most socially desirable residential areas in London should be the Earls Court Road. (If Earls Court Road had an apostrophe, where would it be? Is it the road where one Earl lives or dozens? And which, I wonder, would make it the smarter?) But its take-aways and bed-sits and kangaroo valley immigrants have re-colonised the name completely. Earls Court would not, now, be a good name for a new premium-priced aftershave.

New, earned meanings can invade the emptiest of names. Just say XJ or XK to a serious car person and watch the pupils dilate. (Then say C5 and watch them glaze over again.)

It took me 50 years to realise that the long-established deodorant had been hoping to get us to think 'Odor? O, no!'. It can only be good news for the brand that we don't.

As names, whether initially empty or initially full, simply come to stand for earned brand values, those carefully contrived double meanings get completely lost along the way

In the end, it is context, and only context, that counts. Drive half a mile south from Earls Court and you get to Chelsea. What does Chelsea mean?

Chelsea means the King's Road and swinging London. Chelsea means Stamford Bridge. Chelsea means the President's daughter. Chelsea means pensioners. Chelsea means the flower show. Chelsea means the Chelsea Arts Ball. Chelsea means buns. Context tells us which is which. There's no overlap and, astonishingly, no confusion.

Whatever daughter Lourdes turns out to be like, that's what her name will come to mean; as it would had she been called Winifred or Trixie-Belle. (But not, I grant you, had she been called Odorono.)

What sort of family does this Jaffa cake come from?

An edited version of a speech given to the British Direct Marketing Association in May 1985. Thirteen years on, direct marketing has grown in size and salience – becoming relationship marketing and one-to-one marketing in the process – and the recognition of the value of the corporate brand has also increased. But I see little sign of corporate values being built more commonly into direct marketing campaigns. Since most experts agree that the key to success in future direct marketing – and particularly in electronic commerce – will be the establishment of trust, I find this strange.

I want to take this opportunity to focus on one element of marketing, advertising and business strategy which we all know about and in my view neglect. It applies to conventional marketing through retailers; to the marketing *of* retailers; and, I'd suggest, at least as much to direct marketing.

To make this single point, I want to call as witnesses the Oxford University Press, the coffee spoons at Langan's, Len Heath's new car, a pile of underpants in a street market, the Sinclair C5, Lexington Avenue, the instant custard market, Hugh Johnson, the Bank of Kuwait and high rents in Harley Street.

I'm sure I've already made my point.

On Tuesday of this week I was given lunch at Langan's. My host and I had apparently identical coffee spoons. But when we looked at their backs – and I've no idea why we looked at their backs – his said 'Made in Japan' and mine said 'Made in Taiwan'. His suddenly seemed the better coffee spoon.

Len Heath once sold his share of an advertising agency and bought an Aston Martin. He told me he'd chosen an Aston Martin because of an advertisement he'd read. 'Fancy that,' I said. 'But the point is,' Len said, 'I saw that advertisement when I was 14.'

I was once at an open-air market on a Saturday morning in the North of England. From one stall, a large pile of gents' underpants was selling briskly. The sign behind them read: 'Genuine Marks & Spencers Rejects!'

The cheapest mortgage you could obtain last week, by one-quarter of one per cent, was from the Bank of Kuwait.

My own company's offices in New York are at 466 Lexington Avenue. The owners obtained access to the west, so the building could legitimately be called The Park Avenue Atrium.

All these trivial facts have one thing in common: they illustrate, in one way or another, that *source, parentage, heritage* can and do significantly affect our perceptions of value – up or down. There may or may not be logic or justice in this truth: but truth it is.

The first instant custard to be launched in this country came from Brown & Poulson. It was very successful until the second instant custard came along, from Batchelors. Which was very successful until the third instant custard came along, from Birds. And Birds wiped the floor with both of them.

Where things – objects or services – *come from* matters to us all.

Until very recently, anything from Sinclair was looked at with optimistic respect. I hate to think what the reception of the C5 has done to the authority of the Sinclair name.

A specialist in Harley Street tells you there's nothing wrong with you and sends you a bill for £500. The same man in Surbiton would have been lucky to get away with £50.

In many of the marketing battles of today, everyone is competing for the same money from the same audience. Retailers are competing with their own suppliers with their own brands. Direct marketers are competing with both, and, of course, with each other.

The cry is efficiency. Be a low-cost producer. Enjoy economies of scale, in manufacture and distribution. Pick the

right products. Fulfil fast. Price it right. And of course, these
are all essential conditions for survival, let alone success.

But, *all other things being equal,* the biggest prizes will go to
those marketers, manufacturers or retailers who recognise the
value of *source*; who create such a respect for source that
people will choose *their* products rather than identical
products from an unrespected source or from no source at all.

The balance of power between the retailer's brand and the
manufacturer's brand has been analysed and debated at more
conferences even than the growth of globalism. But if you
come to think of it, retailers have an almost accidental
advantage which many of them are now quite consciously
exploiting to the full. They are perceived as a source. They are
perceived as selectors. They can build a *general* reputation for
a very wide range of goods. Marks & Spencer can add its
authority to goods that range from fresh foods to gents'
underpants. What manufacturer could do that? The greater the
reputation they acquire as a source the less dependent they are
on the niceties of highly competitive pricing; and the healthier
their margins are likely to be.

Some manufacturers have traditionally followed this strategy
as well – but a surprising number haven't. Look at your
newspapers and magazines and television and you will see that
the majority of brands being advertised are still what I will call
orphan brands – because they appear to have no parents. They
have no source. They don't come from anywhere.

Look through the MEAL figures of ten years ago and the
MEAL figures for today and you'll find that few of these
orphan brands are receiving anything like the same level of
media support they once enjoyed. On their own, these lonely
brands simply don't justify it.

But do they really have to be on their own? Can you
imagine a car manufacturer advertising his models but not even
mentioning his company name? If they'd followed that policy,

the Ford Motor Company would have died with the Model-T and Len Heath would never have bought his Aston Martin.

Publishers – some of them – understand this simple truth. The current dictionary battle between Penguin and the Oxford University Press is at least as much a battle between *sources* – which is what the publishers are – as it is between the intrinsic quality and price of the two dictionaries. However comprehensive it was, which of us would put serious personal money behind a dictionary from Mills & Boon?

I find readers' offers interesting – because the newspaper is stretching its authority to something totally different from the traditional purpose of a newspaper. But it can work. I'd be much more likely to order a case of wine at £50 from Hugh Johnson's *Sunday Times* Wine Club than I would from PO Box 173, Loughborough.

This failure to enhance corporate, parental, source values concerns me in conventional retail marketing – and it concerns me in direct marketing as well.

I sense that direct marketing is *so* measurable, *so* quantifiable, *so* accountable – and so immediately so – that the opportunity to build longer-term values into the source of the offers is seldom being seized.

I am not, please note, talking about empty corporate advertising. I am not implying that any sacrifice needs to be made in return on media investment behind any particular product. I am not even talking about range advertising or 'umbrella' advertising.

I just believe that real people – even including you and me – do like to know where things come from. And in many cases, that familiarity and trust and knowledge can be the one discriminator that turns a near miss into a certain sale.

It is also one of the few factors in marketing that is both wholly within your control and costs nothing.

Had you held precisely this conference, chairman, with precisely this programme on precisely this day: and you'd held it not at the Grosvenor House Hotel but at the Edgware Road Assembly Rooms – I wonder just how many delegates you would have attracted?

Why New Labour is better than spray-on socks

Marketing, April 1997

Here is a test question for all advertising and marketing sophisticates. Who said this, and when?

'This use of advertising – to add a subjective value to the product – becomes increasingly important as the trends in our technology lead to competing products becoming more and more the same.'

The answer: James Webb Young, over 70 years ago. And even he was probably not the first to express the thought.

Yet each marketing generation continues to believe that there was, until only very recently, some golden period when all products were not only demonstrably different from each other but also, wondrously, better than each other.

So we try all sorts of dodges in the hope of re-creating this golden age. We employ gap-analysis to identify unsatisfied consumer needs. Stephen King, that most mordant of planners, once employed gap-analysis to identify the absence on our supermarket shelves of left-handed margarine. As the saying goes: there may be a gap in the market; but is there a market in the gap? And when a major multinational client, in all seriousness, invited the agency to put aside all such practicalities as technology and cost and just come up with really unique ideas that would meet genuine consumer needs, the same Stephen King responded with joyful fecundity. Of his long and entertaining list, I remember spray-on socks and bed-making fluid with particular affection.

Next, of course, the R&D team having failed to come up with a functional product discriminator, we turn to the agency account planner and ask her to invent a non-functional one. This leads to a 30-page document, together with tapes and a mood-board, defining the precise and unique brand personality for the thirty-fourth imported lager to be offered to the drinking public. A work of Jesuitical ingenuity, it is wholly unactionable.

Even those who have been most dismissive of Rosser Reeves and his USP continue to behave as if some sort of competitive claim – functional or non-functional – is invariably necessary for competitive success.

In truth, I don't suppose there's ever been a time when competing products were anything but pretty similar: that's why they're competing products. Nor do I think that real people (as opposed to marketing people) even want their competing products to be sharply distinguished. Before getting too carried away with niche marketing, it's worth remembering what a niche is. It's a small hole in a wall: not often the most profitable place to park your brand. As the Labour Party has belatedly realised, if you want to be a mainstream brand, you'd better be in the main stream: and don't worry too much about being distinctive.

The person who understood all this best was the lady in the Persil focus group who said dismissively: 'Of course they're all the same – everybody knows that. It's up to you to decide which is best.'

Understanding Brands Part I
Learning from my aunt and
Bamber Gascoigne

Marketing Business, May 1996

When I was seven years old, I was taken to have tea with the only rich relation we had. As we were about to leave, she reached for her purse, took out five one-pound notes and gave them to me.

I was, at the time, on two shillings a week pocket money. What I held in my hand was one year's gross income.

Then she peered at the notes and said, 'Oh dear. Those two are *very* dirty. I couldn't possibly let you go away with notes like that.' And she took back two of the five one-pound notes – and didn't replace them.

Forty years later, I was trying to find a friend's house in a bit of unknown country. I saw a postman, stopped the car, wound down the window and asked for help. 'Keep going for a bit', he said. 'Then turn left where the phone box used to be.'

In Manchester airport, there's a down escalator that takes you from the arrivals hall to the buses. At the bottom of the elevator, facing you as you descend, there used to be a sign that said: 'Warning. You are approaching the bottom of the escalator. Please face forward.'

Before any of us can make any sort of sense about the nature of brands and brand communications, we need to remember one deeply inconvenient fact: no two people view the same object in exactly the same way. Unless we understand that fact, and then try very hard indeed to see familiar things through the eyes of others, we'll never get brands and brand marketing right.

The unhelpful medical jargon calls it a Theory of Mind; but there seems to be no single word in the English language to describe the ability to see things through other people's eyes. (Nor even a word to describe the *inability*, which is a great deal more common. An acquaintance who is both an ex-classicist and a member of the Royal College of Psychiatrists suggests *anheteropsia*. Neither he nor I believes this is likely to become part of popular currency.) Perhaps the absence of vocabulary is one key reason why this essential skill continues to be under-recognised.

The two pound notes that my aunt was looking at and the two pound notes that I was looking at were, physically, the same pound notes: they were the same product.

My aunt knew exactly what they represented to her – and assumed, as we all too often do, that the way she saw those notes must be the way that everyone, including me, saw those notes. To her, they meant little; and because they were dirty, they meant even less.

To the seven-year-old me, those two pound notes represented five months' income: unimaginable excesses; gluttonous quantities of Crunchies and sherbet fountains, Dandy, Beano, Champion and every other comic published; sheets of balsawood, tubes of balsawood cement; and the new de Havilland Dinky toy.

My aunt was one of the first people I met who failed to understand the difference between a product and a brand.

Many years later, I read about some research conducted in the United States. Two groups of children had been recruited: one from affluent families and one from poor families. All the children from both groups were then asked to draw, from memory, on a piece of paper, a coin – a quarter.

With memories of my aunt still vivid in my mind, I was not in the least surprised by the result. A quarter through the eyes of the poor children was significantly bigger than a quarter through the eyes of the rich children. Same coin; same size;

same levels of familiarity; same *product*. But seen through different eyes – so a different brand.

When I needed to know the way, I chose to ask the postman because I knew he'd be familiar with the district. I hadn't, of course, allowed for the fact that he'd be over-familiar with the district. So he made no attempt to put himself in my place, to see the road ahead through my eyes. He knew where the phone box used to be; it therefore made total sense for him to tell me to turn left there.

Neither my aunt nor the postman would have made good brand managers. Nor would the person who authorised the siting of the notice in Manchester airport.

Good communicators think not just about what they're transmitting but at least as carefully about what others will be receiving. They are seldom the same thing.

Putting yourself in the place of others, striving to see things through other people's eyes: that is the necessary first stage in understanding and managing brands. A product is an objective thing; and a brand is one person's individual and subjective summary of all the satisfactions that product supplies. No two people will see it in exactly the same way.

In *Developing New Brands,* Stephen King wrote: 'A product is something that is made, in a factory. A brand is something that is bought, by a customer.' This thought is expressed so economically that it can sometimes fail to do itself justice – so let me explore it a little.

Thirty-five years ago, the Volkswagen Beetle was selling strongly in many markets around the world. In America, helped by some extremely deft and perceptive advertising from Doyle Dane Bernbach, the Beetle was a witty, wacky, cheap and cheerful European import. It was a fun car, and all the more fun for being ugly. It was the car you gave your son when he graduated from Princeton. It was the car you drove if you wanted people to know that you already had a Pontiac GTO and a Chevrolet Estate. That was the blend of satisfactions delivered by this object to those people in affluent North America, round about 1960.

At exactly the same time, a few thousand miles south in Latin America, there were hundreds and thousands of people saving and scrimping also in the hope of graduating – but not from Princeton. They were hoping to graduate from their bicycle, their moped or their second-hand banger to their first, new, never-owned-by-anyone-else-before car. And the absolute height of their ambitions was a Volkswagen. It was both expensive and luxurious. It would be a symbol to themselves and others of success, of arrival, of the first step on the road to affluence.

In São Paolo Volkswagens were being cleaned and polished and garaged and cherished. In Connecticut they were being left outside to gather yet more chic dirt.

As made in the factory, exactly the same *product*. But *as bought by consumers*, totally different *brands*.

The word brand has become so fashionable over the last 15 years or so that it sometimes seems we've forgotten what it means; we tend, increasingly, to use it interchangeably with product.

Brands have images. Image is really just another word for reputation. The image of a product, like the reputation of a person, belongs not to the product or to the person, but to those of us who are thinking about it.

If images are constructed by individuals – which they are; and if all individuals are different – which they are; and if *what* individuals are has a pronounced effect on how they perceive things – which it does; then it follows that, if there are five million people aware of the existence of a particular brand, there will be some five million quite distinct images of that brand.

And if that's true, which it is, it makes the job of managing brand communications impossible.

Luckily, however, Bamber Gascoigne is at hand to help. A couple of years ago, when he compiled a dictionary of famous people, he was asked how he chose them – because surely there could be no agreed and objective measurement of who was famous and who was not?

And Gascoigne said that of course that was right: but he'd discovered as he worked on the book that he could quite easily decide on inclusion or exclusion by reference to something he called 'a consensus of subjectivity'. And I found, and still find, that this is an invaluable phrase in the understanding of brands.

Each one of millions of people arrives at a set of feelings more or less independently; but which, on examination, turn out to be quite close to each other: so much so, that we begin to deceive ourselves that we have somehow arrived at an objective truth. But we haven't. A shared brand image, like a shared view about Elle MacPherson or Matisse, is not objective: it's a consensus of subjectivity. And that's what brand management should be striving to achieve.

Understanding Brands Part II
Fresh eggs, flying lessons and the creative consumer

Marketing Business, June 1996

Once we understand that everyone creates their own brands in their own heads in their own way, we're half-way to sanity. Now we only have to understand how they do it; and after that, we might even be able to encourage them to arrive not just at a consensus of subjectivity about our brand but even, hallelujah, a consensus quite close to the one we had actually planned for.

The way that people build brands in their heads is the way we form an impression of anything. It is an intensely creative process. We build an image as birds build nests – from scraps and straws we chance upon. We imbue everything about that brand, however trivial, with meaning and significance. We *infer* all the time. We try to make consistent sense of things, because minds dislike inconsistency and dissonance. People build brands in their heads – *whether or not the owners of that brand intend them to.*

Below, identified by Stephen King, are some of the factors – just a few of the scraps and straws – that have an effect on our total impresson of any brand.

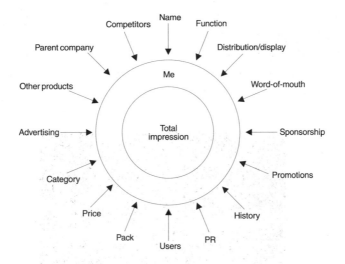

And let me start with function, because I haven't so far given it much attention.

If you present your potential public with a product that is supposed to do something, and it doesn't – or it does it far less well than its competitors – then all the fancy footwork in the world won't save it.

Function should never be taken for granted; function should always be under review; function is at the heart of any brand. But, important as it is, it is no more than a ticket of admission to the stadium. Function entitles you to compete: but in most markets, over time, function alone will not bring sustainable success.

That which makes brands valuable to people, that which makes brands worth more, that which entitles brand owners to decent margins and a good trade presence, is a great, complicated, individually-arrived-at muddle of fact, function and feeling. It is is that muddle, that blend, that synthesis that provides competitively attractive satisfactions to your ultimate users.

And each of these factors – and lots more – will have some effect on each individual's perception of the brand in question.

Please note the ring just before the bull's eye. It says ME

because each one of these factors is filtered through the sub-jective screen: How old am I? How poor? Do I know the brand? Did my mother use it? Does Janey use it? This internal, subconscious self-interrogation is all part of the consumer's creative process.

Here's a real advertisement.

How charming! How primitive and unsophisticated! We professionals find it easy to be loftily indulgent about work of this kind. Some elderly smallholder, eking out his pension, no doubt. He'll probably manage all right as long as he doesn't try to expand.

But imagine if he did, and called in a sophisticated London corporate identity consultancy. It is not wholly impossible – in the interests of modernity and legibility, you understand – that they might recommend their new client to do something like this:

There's been no change of strategy, you will have noticed – nor even of copy.

They might even think it worth testing something along these lines:

Now, as I've repeatedly stressed, all individual responses to common stimuli are different and subjective – so I can't be certain how each of you reading this piece may have responded to those three different advertisements. But I'm reasonably confident that most of you, and indeed most urban egg choosers, would think less well of the eggs offered in the second two advertisements than of those offered in the first.

In fact, of course, if you look back, that original advertisement is a little masterpiece of brand communication. However inadvertently, everything about it triggers the right sort of response: the meticulously hand-lettered sign (but clearly not by a professional art director); not a weed in the flowerbed; the sign not quite straight; the carefully cut grass.

Each of these tiny triggers leads to a rich, internal, coherent composition: a small number of happy, organically-fed, free-range hens looked after personally by a compassionate owner. The word 'fresh' here is redundant: how could they be anything else? Whereas in the second two examples, the typography has not only decided to fight the word 'fresh': it has comprehensively won.

The great skill in designing brand communications is in

selecting those tiny triggers, because those that are uniquely right for one brand will by definition be wrong for another. Here is another brand looking for your custom:

I have repeatedly said that consumers'/receivers' interpretation of brand stimuli is creative. This sign says, factually and accurately, what service is on offer. And that's all it says.

But what does it *imply*? What does it *communicate*? A very, very old flying instructor? A very, very old aircraft? A grass landing-strip with molehills? Decomposing World War II tarmac? Not much maintenance? An open cockpit? Again, each of you will have constructed a slightly different internal mental picture. But I don't think many of you – however irrationally – would have chosen this brand. You may indeed have arrived at a consensus of subjectivity.

A bit of boring old Helvetica here would not have come amiss.

Unless you're launching an absolutely new brand – a brand without even any declared corporate parentage – you will never be in the business of designing communications for empty heads. Each member of your audience will already have views, feelings and prejudices: and you'd better face them fearlessly.

There is still a school of business which I call the Ostrich School of Marketing and its great advantage is simplicity. You start by conducting vast quantities of research that proves incontrovertibly that the entire population believes British Rail to be inefficient, dirty, expensive and self-satisfied. This information is invaluable: not because it prompts management to do anything, but because, with an effortless inversion, it forms the basis of the creative brief. Consumer proposition: British Rail is fast, clean and caring. You may confidenly look forward to a strapline suggesting, for example, that 'This is the age of the train'.

If your aim is to achieve a radical change of brand reputation in the minds of your audience, be at least respectful of what's there already. Remember that every stimulus will have some effect on consumer perceptions, not just the advertising. Remember that your audience will not be judging you absolutely, but relatively: against their own existing feelings and – as always – against your competition.

Don't forget the power of packs and pack designs. A pack is more than something that stands out on the shelf and can be stacked efficiently on pallets. A pack is the face of a brand. And faces tell people whether other people are cold or warm, snobbish or neighbourly, fierce or gentle. The face – the pack – can even influence the way a product is perceived to function.

Many years ago, some excellent research was done for a washing-powder. Like much good pack research, it pretended not to be. There were no tachistoscopes and no preferences sought for alternative designs. Instead, two large samples, one of users and one of non-users, were each given six weeks' supply of two different washing-powder recipes: and they were asked to use both and report back as to which was the more efficient. Nothing else: just which, in use, was better for problem washes.

From both samples came a significant preference for the same version: Version B was clearly the more efficient. In fact, of course, the powder inside the two packs was identical, as were the washing instructions. The only variable was the pack design. Pack A had two little girls on the front and pack B had two little boys on the front.

And to those mothers, or at least to enough of those mothers, there was a clear and important distinction between boy-dirt and girl-dirt. Girls got dirty but boys got absolutely bloody filthy. It followed that any washing powder that set out to deal with boy-dirt was likely to be more efficacious. None of this, of course, happened in such a plodding manner or at such a conscious level – but that's, in practice, as they compared the two, what those respondents found to be the case.

Understanding Brands Part III
Madonna, the Harvard Business Review and the second law of thermodynamics

Marketing Business, July 1996

When trying to communicate brand benefits and brand values, there's an understandable and sometimes overwhelming desire to get your message across; to spell it out; to say it several times; to sing it as well as say it; to super it up at the end: above all, to be *explicit.*

Any form of communication is a blend of the sender implying and the receiver inferring. If you hope that by being explicit you eliminate misconceptions and ambiguity, you will be disappointed. The more involving the communication, the greater the proportion of inference; which is why, when the receiver infers, and when the inference is that which you had hoped and planned for, the communication will be many times more effective.

In his difficult book, *The Act of Creation*, Arthur Koestler wrote: 'Language itself is never completely explicit. Words have suggestive, evocative powers; but at the same time they are merely stepping stones for thought. The artist rules his subjects by turning them into accomplices.'

Like it or not, your receivers are not passive, but active; and tirelessly creative in the way that they interpret your signals. So it must make sense to harness that creativity rather than try to bludgeon it into passivity; to try, in other words, to turn your receivers into accomplices. (See *The consumer has a mind as well as a stomach*, p 115.)

Apart from relevance, salience and relentless monitoring of functional performance, what else does a strong brand need? What else is it that allows a brand to sustain decent margins, withstand competitive onslaughts and make monkeys of all product life cycle theorists?

For me, the best way to understand the nature of brand strength is through metaphor and analogy.

The bleak truth about our physical world is that it doesn't stand still. It's in a constant state of running down, of getting colder. That is the natural state of things; and that is the natural state of established brands.

The value that strong brands have to their users can usefully be seen as a sort of warmth. People can cup their hands round them and, like cats on a boiler, enjoy being close to them.

The second law of thermodynamics, very roughly, says this: when two objects touch, and their temperatures are different, heat will flow from the warmer to the cooler until their temperatures are equalised.

Apply that back to brands. Established brands, like the earth itself, if left to themselves, grow cooler all the time. That is the natural state of things. And whenever we ask a brand to add its lustre and authority to sub-brands, line-extensions and variants, we're quite deliberately setting out to drain it of some of the very warmth that made it of value to people in the first place. The second law of thermodynamics will ensure that brand temperatures between master-brand and sub-brand begin to equalise; and so the master-brand, the source of all our market strength, our resistance to competition, our strongest card against the retail trade and our most reliable profit contributor, gets cooler.

Fewer and fewer free-standing brands are being launched; it's too expensive. More and more existing brands are being asked to foster sub-brands; it's cheaper.

And the reason it's cheaper is because we're deliberately drawing on the capital warmth of a brand we've already created – or, more probably, inherited.

Asking established brands to sponsor sub-brands is not wrong. What's wrong is to underestimate the risk and the cost.

The ideal, of course, is for all brand extensions to be such a good fit with the original, and of such intrinsic interest, that within months they are bestowing new warmth on their parents.

If the natural state of things is for established brands to lose their warmth, and if they're constantly being drained still further of that warmth to help advance our expansionist ambitions, how do we stop them petering out altogether like some expended meteorite?

At the heart of any strong and resilient brand lies a sort of fame. When things and people are famous, they can earn more money. This may not be fair or noble, but it's true. Max Clifford and other notorious publicists know it, and we should study them with interest.

I am not, of course, saying that if a brand is famous, that's all it has to worry about. But without the maintenance of fame, and quite a broad and catholic form of fame at that, a master-brand's core warmth will be slowly, immeasurably and perhaps irretrievably dissipated. And for that fame to be of the greatest value, a brand must be known to an audience far wider than the normal, meticulous media planner would specify.

Of the millions of people who know about Madonna, perhaps one per cent will ever go to a concert and five per cent buy a record. Yet the value to Madonna and her brand managers of that other 95 per cent is incalculable. It seems to be in the nature of real fame that it needs to be indiscriminate.

All this has considerable implications for communications strategy and the need to understand the difference between the values of private media and the values of public media.

Direct marketing – database marketing, one-to-one marketing, relationship marketing – is on the increase; and deservedly so, since it's being closely monitored and it's clearly earning its keep. It does much to personalise the brand/consumer relationship; and it also goes a long way towards the elimination of waste, since the money is spent on developing existing relationships, not broadcasting wildly to the uninterested majority.

Direct marketing is a very *private* medium: that is its strength. But is it enough – *on its own* – to build and sustain brands? If we accept that brands need fame, can one-to-one marketing, on its own, deliver?

Virgin and Richard Branson have realised, in both senses of the word, the value to Virgin of simple fame and they've certainly been users of direct marketing; but the fame that Virgin now enjoys has come mainly from public media: from advertising, public relations, sponsorship, hot-air ballooning and many other headline-grabbing stunts. And their fame is now so strong and so general that it can add value and interest to music and air travel and holidays and cola and vodka and even financial services. They are known to millions of people who may never be in the market for a Virgin product. Is this, then, wasteful?

I believe not. I believe they add immeasurably to Virgin's corporate brand strength. And I also believe, with a wonderful irony, that at exactly the time when media developments may theoretically make it possible for us to eliminate waste, we may finally come to see that it has never in truth been waste.

This is not, please note, an attack on the new media; they are welcome. But there's a sort of hysteria that overcomes commentators at moments of change; an assumption that there can be no middle course; that a new medium will either fail completely, or be attracting 110 per cent of all advertising revenue within five years.

It is true that no successful new advertising medium has ever left existing media undisturbed; but neither has any existing medium ever been totally displaced.

There will be many ways to create and develop a brand's profitability, but one of them will continue to be the maintenance of its brand warmth through public media: maybe advertising, maybe PR, maybe sponsorship, maybe stunts.

The category of advertising that most baffles and antagonises social commentators is that for established brands. They do not understand why it is necessary for a brand that is well known to everyone and has been sampled by most to continue to spend millions of pounds on promotion. Many marketing companies are a little bit baffled, too. They start each year with objectives set in terms of growth – of volume or share or margin – which they frequently fail to meet.

But then think of brand warmth. Think of a brand as a night storage heater, needing regular re-charging if it is to maintain its appeal. It becomes a perfectly legitimate annual decision to allocate marketing money to the maintenance of brand warmth; because the alternative is to see brand potency decline and with it, future margins and future brand development.

It is now 41 years since the *Harvard Business Review* published Gardner and Levy's 'The Product and the Brand': perhaps the first authoritative analysis of the nature of brands. Much of what they wrote is now accepted as self-evident, but some still isn't. The contribution of advertising (publicity, saliency, fame) to established brands is still not universally understood.

They wrote: 'a single campaign is not the manufacturer's only salesman, and he usually intends to remain in business for many following years. From this point of view, it is more profitable to think of an advertisement as a contribution to the complex symbol which is the brand image – as part of the *long-term investment in the reputation of the brand.*' (Their italics.)

Madonna, Max Clifford, Richard Branson and most grown-up marketing companies would probably agree; but it's odd that the point has still to be made.

Marketing 1948: how easy it was – just like Wembley

Marketing, June 1996

I haven't read them all, of course, so I may be wrong. But I believe it to be the case that every single marketing strategy written since 1955 contains the sentence: 'It is essential that we recognise the increasing sophistication of our consumers.' Every year, for at least 40 years, in compound leaps, consumers have been growing more and more sophisticated. Where, I sometimes wonder, will it all end?

The precise nature of this escalating sophistication is never specified, but day-to-day observation eliminates most alternatives. It can't mean better-mannered or more chicly dressed or more suavely articulate. So it can only mean smart. In other words, less gullible. In other words, less easy to sell things to.

And all at once, the reason for this annual sophistication warning becomes clear. What we're really saying is: hey, this is getting difficult. They're getting very stroppy out there. These days they're all marketing literate and icon-saturated and can spot the flaws in the rural image through a one-way mirror. So don't be surprised if this re-launch bombs, know what I'm saying?

It's never actually said, but there's often a hint of regret about all this: an unspoken nostalgia for the good old days when all you had to do was tell the peasants to go out and buy something and, with a deferential touch to the flat cap or a bob of the bonnet, they would obediently do so. Consumers, in those days, knew their place. They'd been put on this earth to consume and that, with touching gratitude, is precisely what they did. How easy – how very, very easy – it must have been in marketing before all this sophistication set in.

I haven't read them all, of course, so I may be wrong. But I believe it to be the case that every single advertising brief written since 1955 contains the sentence: 'Given the intensified competition in the marketplace, we expect our advertising to work even harder for us in the coming fiscal.'

Every year, relentlessly, the job of the advertising agency gets more and more difficult. How easy it must have been – how very, very easy – when advertising briefs read: 'Given our product's significant price advantage and the buoyant state of the market as a whole, little if any contribution will be expected from our advertising in the coming fiscal.'

There are, I expect, athletes preparing for Atlanta who wish they were going to Wembley. How easy it must have been – how very, very easy – to win the 100 metres back in 1948.

It's a puzzling form of self-deception, this. Comparisons across time are meaningless. Winning things gets neither harder nor easier. The increased sophistication of your consumers, real or imagined, will affect your competitors no less than yourself. There has never been a time when advertising was expected to do anything other than work hard.

To the envious practitioners of 2040, marketing in the 1990s will presumably seem to have been a doddle. How easy, they will think, how very, very easy.

The reason it doesn't seem so now is because it isn't.

3
How advertising works

The consumer has a mind as well as a stomach

Being the creative director in an advertising agency means spending a great deal of time discussing and evaluating work done by others. Much of the development work you are shown seems wrong; either strategically wrong or executionally wrong. When it is strategically wrong, it is relatively easy to explain why you want it changed but when you feel the execution is at fault, the problem becomes a great deal harder. It never seemed satisfactory – or fair – simply to say, 'This isn't good enough, start again'. I always felt the need to try to explain why; to try to relate the specific rejection to a more general principle. In this way, disappointments could at least be part of a learning process – and besides, it was good for me to try to explain and justify my decision. The problem was, there were (and are) few sensible and articulated theories about how advertising works. There are some 'rules', some sets of beliefs about what is good or bad: but very little communications theory, however inadequate, on which to build and against which to test a particular instinct about a particular proposal. Again and again I found myself having to explain that *saying* something did not mean that you had communicated it; and almost as often, that not having said something didn't necessarily mean that you had *not* communicated it. The first time I put these thoughts together in public was in 1972 to a Kraft International Management Conference in Switzerland. Despite the fact that I took an unconscionable time to get to the point and then failed to make it very skilfully, the presentation is reproduced here more or less exactly as I first gave it. In various forms and under various titles (most commonly 'Stimulus & Response'), the basic thought continued to be usefully (and better) expressed both by me and many others in the agency for at least the next 15 years. Sadly, not all those who claimed to espouse the theory understood it: a fact only too evident when they came to talk about it. A much more disciplined version of this original, without illustrations, appeared in *Admap* in 1985 under the title 'Getting explicit about the implicit'. I am grateful to Terry Hamaton for devising and producing the illustrations for this chapter.

If you work on the creative side in an advertising agency, you get an extremely clear picture of what advertising is all about. Or, to be more precise, you get two very clear pictures.

The first is the one you get from listening to strangers at parties, from serious television programmes (particularly on the BBC) and from books written by intelligent people with a genuine concern for human values. This picture is, at least in some ways, extremely flattering.

I learn from these people that, as a maker of advertisements, I have unlimited and infallible powers of persuasion. I can create needs where none previously existed. I can manipulate and motivate, perfectly and pervasively. I can accept the assignment of selling a worthless new product at a premium price and guarantee success. I can drive innocent people to such an uncontrollable frenzy of desire that they will begin using deodorants when they don't even smell and buy two cars before they've learned to drive. I can sell a toxic lipstick by equating it with love, create bankrupts with a single slogan and hypnotise all humanity, like lemmings, into a suicidal rush to consume the unnecessary and the unhealthy.

That, according to these people, is the power that I have: and pretty heady stuff it is.

And then, the following morning, I go to a client meeting.

Last year's advertising budget was 15 per cent up. The product has been proved to be significantly preferred to its main competitors. Distribution is good, the price is fair, trade margins and incentives are favourable and the sales force is well trained, enthusiastic and large. Yet the sales of the product are eight and a half per cent down.

Now – why should this be? The most senior client looks at the most junior client. The junior client looks at the most senior agency man. The senior agency man looks at the account executive. And the account executive looks at me.

It is perfectly clear to everyone why the sales are eight and a half per cent down. The advertising isn't any good.

Now at times like this, as I'm sure you'll understand, I get a little resentful. There are all these people staring at me, as if it were all my fault. They don't realise, all these clients and senior agency people, that I'm a man of unlimited and infallible powers of persuasion.

Why don't they go to the parties that I go to? They'd soon come to realise that advertising is *always* successful – whatever the product and its price. They'd soon realise that, skilfully advertised, not only will a brand automatically increase its market share every year, but so will *every* brand in that market, too.

There is, of course, only one way to explain this phenomenon, this extraordinary discrepancy between these two different pictures of advertising.

The critics of advertising know that consumers can be *made* to consume in ever increasing quantities. Advertisers *want* consumers to consume in ever increasing quantities. Agencies do their best to *persuade* consumers to consume in ever increasing quantities. And yet, only too often, they don't.

The blame, then, lies inescapably at the feet of the consumer. I'm afraid it has to be said: the consumer of today is quite frequently guilty of gross irresponsibility. 'Look here,' I sometimes feel like saying to them, 'you're a consumer, aren't you? Then why the hell aren't you out there consuming?'

Advertising has never been without its critics. It never will be and it never should be. From time to time, however, the criticism changes in both nature and force; and this seems to be such a time in many countries of the world.

The criticism comes from many quarters and is of many kinds. I don't intend, nor am I at all qualified, to deal with all of these today. Nor do I intend, particularly to this audience, to put the case for advertising: except to say that the longer I work in the business and the more I think about it, the more certain I become that the general effect of advertising is overwhelmingly for the public good. Ralph Nader once said that, in his opinion, power can be exercised responsibly only so long as it remains insecure. I know of no company, particularly no company such as yours, which is totally dependent for survival and profit on the public's acceptance of the goods it offers, that feels even close to total security for more than a week or two at a time. The whole structure of the competitive system precludes security, complacency and abuse of power. If anything, perhaps, we feel more insecure than we need or should.

But there's one specific facet of advertising criticism that I would like to consider this afternoon and for two reasons.

First, it happens to interest me a great deal, and I long ago came to the conclusion that it is on the whole preferable for at least the speaker to be interested in his subject, even if his audience is not.

The second reason is that I believe there is some substance to this particular area of criticism; that we, advertiser and agency, *can* do something about it; and that, in so doing, we can actually produce and publish more effective advertisements.

It's difficult to define this area precisely; but the phrase most often used, in both the US and the UK, by commentators and consumers alike is that much advertising is *'an insult to the intelligence'.*

Now if it is true that some of the very consumers we wish to influence feel insulted and irritated by the advertising we produce, then it seems a subject worthy of a little thought. For example, what precisely is meant by 'an insult to the intelligence'? Does any advertisement, inevitably, have an irritant factor? Is there any correlation between irritating advertising and effective advertising? And if so, is that correlation negative or positive?

I can't, I'm afraid, promise to give definitive answers to any of those questions; but I would like to put forward a theory, a hypothesis, that may be of interest to you. And I'd like to begin by talking, not about advertising at all, but about the whole nature of communications.

If you read books about communication, you'll find that many of them break the communications process down into four different component parts.

There's a Sender:

A Receiver:

A Medium:

And a Message:

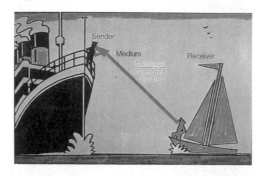

The man in the big boat says to the man in the little boat: 'Get out of my way!' The little man does, and the communication has been successfully completed. It all seems very simple, doesn't it? But let's see how the same principle applies to other forms of communication.

Here's another sender:

The advertiser. He, too, has his receivers, his potential customers:

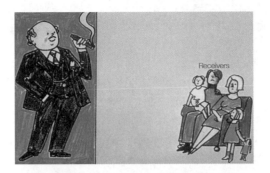

Again, there's a medium – in this case, television:

Now what about the message? Well, that's not particularly difficult, because the advertiser knows exactly what he wants the consumer to do. He wants the consumer to buy his product. So the message, obviously, is: 'Buy my product'.

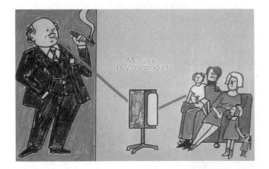

You may think this is slightly unfair and that not much advertising these days is quite so blatant and aggressive in its tone. But if you read your newspapers and watch your television, you'll still see and hear a lot of advertising which says: 'This product is the best' or 'Buy some today'.

The main question arising here is this: if the man in the little boat gets out of the way of the man in the big boat, why doesn't the consumer invariably buy the product when he's been told clearly and forcibly by the advertiser that he should?

Now: either we return to the conclusion that all consumers are irresponsible and should be subject to heavy fines if they don't do what they're told, or we look for some other explanation.

To help us let's look at yet another communicator:

This particular sender is meant to be a comedian, a funnyman. He, too, has his receivers:

In this instance, a typical British family on a Saturday night out, determined under no circumstances to enjoy themselves. The comedian's medium, of course, is his voice.

But what's his message? Well, he knows what he wants his receivers to think, all right. He wants them to think he's funny. But I very much doubt if any comedian, at least more than once, would get up on the stage and begin by saying: 'Ladies and Gentlemen:

The first thing I think you should know about me is that I am funny.'

The comedian is a far more skilful communicator than that. He knows that if that audience is to think he's funny, then he's got to make them laugh; he has to tell them what we call a joke.

So he tells the joke, and the audience laughs. It is *their response* that he's funny. *They* come to that conclusion: it's their contribution, not the comedian's:

And it's this illustration, I believe, that begins to cast serious doubt on the normal communications model of sender, receiver, medium and message. The real flaw in that theory is that it *in no way allows for participation or contribution by the receiver.*

And like it or not, all receivers do participate. They resolutely refuse to sit there with minds like empty sponges, accepting all that they're told without question or modification. For example, at the moment, I'm a sender; and you, unfortunately for you, are receivers. Supposing I told you in all seriousness that I was a man of many remarkable qualities but that probably my *most* remarkable quality was one of modesty. 'I'd like you to know,' I would say, 'that I'm an extremely modest man.'

Well: that, you could argue, was my message. 'I am an extremely modest man.' But do you accept it? Do I see you turning to each other and murmuring respectfully: 'What a modest man! Did you hear him tell us he was modest? I never knew before that he was modest!'

I suggest you don't. I suggest that, in fact, you arrive at a diametrically opposite conclusion. You conclude that my most pronounced characteristic is that, not of modesty, but of conceit.

And so it can be in advertising. A message which was foolish enough, for example, to proclaim: 'Volkswagen: the *spacious* car' would almost certainly elicit the response: 'It bloody isn't.'

This theory is given academic respectability by a Spanish professor – Professor Aranguren – who has this to say in his book *Human Communications:* 'The emission does not always and inevitably lead to the simple, quiet and passive reception of a message, but frequently excites an active response: and for the same reason, this response may be in opposition to the emission instead of conforming with it.'

But with due respect to the good professor, I don't think he's got it absolutely right even yet – because he's still using this word 'message'.

Increasingly it seems to me that 'message' and 'promise' and 'proposition' are very dangerous words. They are dangerous because we use them to stand for two quite different things, and we don't always distinguish between them. Sometimes we use the word 'message' to mean what we *put into* communication; sometimes to mean what the receiver *takes out.* And however inconvenient and untidy it may be, we have to realise that these two can be, and indeed almost always are, different. I *put in*: 'I am modest.' You *take out*: 'He is conceited.'

It seems to me, therefore, that the communications chain is not, in truth, made up of those four accepted component parts: sender, receiver, medium and message. It is made up of five, and the five are these:

Sender:

Receiver:

Medium:

Stimulus:

Response:

And the key words here are 'stimulus' and 'response', which replace the single word 'message'. As advertisers, we are the senders. It is tempting to believe that our job is to 'give the consumer the message'. But it isn't – it's rather more subtle than that.

Our job is, first, to decide on the response we would like our receivers to contribute. And second, to determine what particular stimuli are likely to evoke that response.

It is with considerable diffidence that one looks at another country's political situation, let alone makes any comment on it. But, to me, political persuasion is a fascinating subject from which much can be learned.

A great deal of party political propaganda is vicious, personal, ruthless. By comparison, it makes the battle between rival detergent manufacturers seem like a Darby and Joan Club meeting.

There was one particularly famous – or perhaps notorious – political advertisement which was published some years ago in the States. I couldn't get a reference for the original, but it showed a photograph of a dark-jowled and shify-looking Richard Nixon and underneath it said:

'Would you buy a used car from this man?'

Now, whatever you may feel about the ethics of this sort of propaganda, it seems like a masterly piece of communication.

The desired response was to cast doubt on Mr Nixon's integrity. But the advertisement didn't simply say; 'This man is dishonest' – which could well have provoked an immediate sympathy for Mr Nixon. The advertisers realised that the receivers, the wavering Republicans, should be invited to make that contribution for themselves. 'Would you buy a used car from this man?' is not a message: it is a stimulus. It recognises that receivers do not receive with empty heads. It recognises that people will always relate what they are told to what they think they already know. In this case, what they believed they knew was that all used car salesmen are devious, dishonest and untrustworthy.

So the conclusion one is forced to reach is the conclusion reached by Arthur Koestler in his book *The Act of Creation.*

He says: 'Language itself is never completely explicit. Words have suggestive, evocative powers; but at the same time they are merely stepping-stones for thought. The artist rules his subjects by turning them into accomplices.'

That seems to me as good a definition of the role of the creative man in advertising as I've ever read. We have to try to rule our subjects by turning them into accomplices; because if they aren't accomplices, they may well turn out to be enemies.

Let me now try to summarise where I think I've got to.

— Many people – our consumers – find much advertising irritating: and if anything, this trend is on the increase. Some of this irritation is undoubtedly caused by the weight of advertising, by the intensity of advertising, by repetition and by the irrelevance of certain groups of products to certain groups of people. It's not altogether surprising, for example, that many men find detergent advertising the most irritating of all, since they neither buy nor use the products advertised. [*Still true in 1998.*]

— On the other hand, some, at least, of this irritation springs from advertisements which people describe as being 'an insult to their intelligence'.

— What this particular phrase seems to mean is not simply talking down to people or hectoring people. It means that the sender has an inadequate understanding of the communications process in general and the role of the receiver in particular.

— The receiver is not passive: he is active. He will contribute, complete, modify, reject or repudiate: whether we like it or not. *He doesn't absorb messages: he responds to stimuli.* He draws his own conclusions.

— If we attempt to deny the receiver the chance to contribute, we run the risk not only of failing to achieve satisfactory communication, but also of irritating him a great deal into the bargain.

I've left one question deliberately unanswered. If you can't *tell* people what to do; if you've got to rule your subjects by

turning them into accomplices; then why did this work?
Why did the man in the little boat get out of the way of the man in the big boat?

The answer, of course, is that he had to; because if he hadn't, he'd have been dead. That provides a motivation more powerful than those normally available to advertisers. This sort of communication is essentially fascist in nature; it depends for its success on the ability of the sender to penalise the receiver quite severely if he obstinately refuses to obey the instruction. It's the communications equivalent of gunboat diplomacy.

The advertiser is never in such a position of power. He is always less powerful than the sum of his potential customers. The advertiser who behaves as though he were in possession of such power will regret it bitterly on two counts. First, he will be making less than optimum use of his advertising money; and second, he will not only bring down on his head the wrath of the vocal, minority consumerist groups, but he will annoy and irritate and fail to persuade the very people on whom he depends for success and profit.

I've spent a long time this afternoon expounding this theory. I came to realise about ten days ago that it is possible to make the point just as effectively in less than a minute. Someone showed me a cartoon from *The New Yorker Magazine* – you may have seen it:

"From here it's just a bunch of stripes and stars. It doesn't say '*America*.'"

'From here it's just a bunch of stripes and stars. It doesn't *say* America.'

(Drawing by Weber; © 1972, *The New Yorker Magazine*, Inc.)

A new neurosis: too many people may be seeing your advertising

Marketing, December 1995

Here is a very short seasonal quiz.

Question: What does gift advertising have in common with Michael Portillo, June Whitfield and the Labour Party?

Answer: They all have multiple audiences.

I once saw a notice on the outside window of an extremely pretentious restaurant which read: 'Staff Wanted. No Experience Necessary.' If I'd fancied a go at being a wine-waiter at *Chez Gourmet*, I'd have been pleased by this news. As someone who was thinking of eating there, I wasn't.

Even after 30 years, political parties still haven't worked out how to deal with television cameras at party conferences. The audience in the hall, the party faithful, united in their allegiance and emboldened by their numbers, is ready for more or less anything as long as it's unreasonable. Labour leaders at the Sheffield rally just before the 1992 election gave them premature triumphalism. Michael Portillo at the last Conservative conference gave them a heady whiff of xenophobia. On both occasions, the audience in the hall became inflamed with love and eternal commitment.

But the cameras were also there, snooping and eavesdropping and relaying these hot responses to another audience at home. And the audience at home was altogether cooler: remote and heterogeneous; composed of many hundreds of thousands of small, sceptical, half-attentive domestic units. The audience at home loved neither the Labour leaders nor Mr Portillo. Stoically uninflamed, they registered instead severe disapproval. And between them they accounted for a great many votes.

Both the Labour Party and Mr Portillo learned the hard way that you forget about multiple audiences at your cost.

Convenience foods had already learnt it. They used to think that their only audience was buyers and servers: 'Makes a dishonest woman of you' promised the domestic caterer that she could get away with it; but the promise was made in front of the family, the eaters, the real consumers. These days most convenience foods wisely take their convenience for granted and go all out on quality. Quality's of interest to all audiences – another lesson, perhaps, for Mr Portillo.

And then we have gifts.

Gifts are different from every other purchase we make. Gifts have only one initial function: to occupy the space within a parcel. We buy gifts not because we want them but because we want to get rid of them.

The point of giving is to earn gratitude and affection. We want recipients to open our parcel and look at us with wondrous, shining pleasure. We want them to think that we have been imaginative and thoughtful; that only we, in our sensitive, perceptive way, could have conceived of that particular present for that particular person.

So why then, I sometimes wonder, does anybody ever choose something that's been advertised as an acceptable gift ten times an evening on national television since early October? And even more puzzlingly: why do some peddlars of gifts put all their emphasis on how astonishingly cheap their products are?

I can only suppose, like Mr Portillo and *Chez Gourmet*, they've forgotten about that other audience.

Don't shoot the packshot!

Marketing, July 1995

It's a pity that packshots are called packshots. The word reminds you what they are but stops you understanding what they do. So the age-old comic debate continues: clients want them in and preferably big; art directors want them small and preferably out. A compromise is reached. The packshot is included: big enough to disrupt the original script or layout (which had excluded it altogether) but too small to be of value. The daily evidence is there in every medium, perhaps most reprehensibly in posters.

There are lots of different kinds of packshot, many of which aren't packshots at all, but they all fulfil one central, priceless function. As David Ogilvy wrote 45 years ago, every exposure of every good advertisement makes an important if often immeasurable contribution to the competitive personality of the brand it features. Over time, these tiny, cumulative contributions can hugely enhance the distinction of the brand – but only if they are stored. And where they like to be stored is in some constant, visual symbol.

It may be the pack itself; it may be a logo or an emblem (Michelin man or Andrex puppy); it may be consistent typography (Lloyds Bank, Tiffany's, Volkswagen); it may be the Rolls-Royce radiator. Occasionally, though rarely, it's not visual at all but a snatch of music or a distinctive voice.

Whatever the form, the purpose is common: to act as a receptacle for the brand's values; to be a rechargeable dry-cell battery which – like any battery – does two things. It accepts and holds a charge; and it releases that charge on demand. Again like any battery, its physical state is one of natural decay: it can't be left for long without recharging.

All new symbols start empty. Over time, and in the hands of skilful brand management, they take on meanings, values and associations – absorbed, cumulatively, from the contexts in which they appear. A fully-charged brand symbol, in the flicker of an eye, can re-transmit brand values that may have taken years to foster. And the advertising in which that symbol appears is simultaneously both exposing and recharging it.

None of this has much to do with on-shelf pack recognition. I have heard senior marketing persons speak solemnly of the need to increase the size of the packshot so that the aisle-cruising housewife is more likely to recognise the pack that she's had in her kitchen for the last 15 years. With fans like this, no wonder the packshot is held in such contempt by equally senior agency people.

Packshots are mugshots: they're the face of the brand. They're flags, they're football strip, they're anthems. When we see them, all the good feelings we've accumulated in our minds are instantly refreshed and released.

The best advertising for repeat-purchase brands works both immediately and over time. It both generates extra sales and, at least as importantly, keeps the brand's batteries perpetually charged.

To leave out a packshot is to condemn each advertisement to remain just that: a single, discrete and transitory ad. It will never play a bigger, longer role. It will never repay its cost. It will never be part of advertising.

What Jim Young said. And what he didn't say

James Webb Young practised, taught and wrote about advertising for 50 years. For the whole of that time he either worked for, or was a consultant to, J. Walter Thompson. So much of what he taught and wrote had such a timeless sanity about it that I took to using his work – particularly *How To Become an Advertising Man* – as a basis for internal training. The following piece started life in 1978 as a presentation, with a great many illustrative examples of advertising, to a meeting held in Majorca of J. Walter Thompson European managers. As in the title, the book employs the masculine throughout. This is not because Jim Young wrote it exclusively for men, or believed men more suited to advertising than women. Indeed, he worked closely for much of his life with Helen Resor, an outstanding copywriter and a great encourager of women in advertising. As was common at the time, he employed the masculine to represent both genders.

I'm taking as my text today Jim Young's book *How to Become an Advertising Man*. I suspect that most of you know it well and will have read it more than once. What I *don't* know is what proportion of all the people working in J. Walter Thompson offices around the world have read it – or even heard of it: but if the London office is any guide, I suspect the proportion is fairly small, such as one per cent.

I believe Jim Young was one of the more remarkable advertising men, and that this particular book is one of the best – and shortest and simplest – ever written on the subject by anyone, anywhere. What's more, he's *ours:* and arguably, second only to Stanley Resor, he was more responsible than anyone else for building the company and its reputation around the world.

It is *not* my intention to canonise Jim Young: to give him the kind of papal infallibility that some members of Ogilvy & Mather seem determined to confer on their remarkable but fallible founder. Nor is this talk more than a first attempt to see if, in Jim Young, we might not have an important and under-utilised resource that could help us professionally.

We have often, as a company, been proud of the fact that we were once described as 'the university of advertising'. And I suspect, particularly over the last ten years or so, we have tried more systematically than most agencies to pass on knowledge, to think about theory and to generalise as well as practise – and to encourage those theories and generalisations to be questioned, modified, invalidated and improved.

Yet, unlike proper universities and more easily defined disciplines, there is a curious lack of agreed theory or accumulated knowledge on the subject of advertising. We often complain that everybody thinks they're an expert in advertising: whether they're consumerists, bureaucrats, people we meet at parties, consumers themselves or 23-year-old brand managers. But perhaps we make it all too easy for these varied groups to see themselves as experts – simply because we aren't expert ourselves. The mere fact that someone has worked in an advertising agency for a few years, with little or no formal training or education in the subject, does not, in my view, entitle that person to believe himself or herself to be an expert.

So my main objective, in redirecting our minds and attention to Jim Young's book, is not that we should stop thinking for ourselves and just accept without question or modification what the man said, but more to identify one of the rare pieces of clearly expressed advertising philosophy and use it as a kind of historical fix. What *was* he saying and doing and writing between 1912 and 1964? Are there any obvious truths and guidelines we've forgotten? Have we added anything since, and if so, what? And can a good, hard, respectful look back help us look forward – and be better at what we do than we currently are?

As Jim Young says in the Preface to his book: 'Becoming an Advertising Man is a life-long process. I have been engaged in it for over 50 years, and still see no end to the road.' And that wasn't just false modesty; he knew that to be true and of course it still is.

He goes on to define, in Chapter 1, what he means by the term Advertising Man: 'The true Advertising Man, as the term is used in this book, is he who has the knowledge, skills, experience and insights to advise advertisers how best to use advertising to accomplish their objectives. *And* to execute the advertising to do this.'

Now, I've called this talk 'What Jim Young said. And what he didn't say' because I find that what he takes for granted, what is implicit – in other words, what he *doesn't* say – is at least as illuminating as what he *does*. And this definition is a good example.

For as long as I can remember, we've put great emphasis in this company on the account group, or planning group, or project team. Certainly it has been agreed that the account man should be ultimately responsible for the output and the success of that group – but we never expect him to be good at everything. Jim Young makes no such assumptions. He talks about the Advertising Man as an *individual*.

In Chapter III, he picks up the word 'knowledge', that which he believes the advertising individual should try to acquire, and defines it as follows:

1. Knowledge of propositions

2. Knowledge of markets

3. Knowledge of messages

4. Knowledge of carriers of messages

5. Knowledge of trade channels

6. Knowledge of how advertising works

7. Knowledge of the specific situation

He recounts how one young man responded to this list by saying 'Sounds to me as though only God Almighty could ever meet all the requirements.'

Young goes on to say: 'If you should have any such feeling, let me hasten to point out that in the practice of advertising today you will find yourself supported by specialists in many phases of these different categories, and will have at hand many tools in the way of reference books, and many developed techniques for acquiring current facts.'

So, while he is certainly conceding that help is, and should be, available to the Advertising Man, he is still not talking about a group or a team. He goes on to say: 'There is a very considerable range of knowledge in all these categories with which you must become familiar, and some of which you must master.'

So the first question I'd like to leave hanging in the air is this: 'Has the growth of the concept of the account group, composed of so-called specialists in media, creativity and planning, quite unintentionally made the existence of the complete Advertising Man less likely? What, today, is the role of the account executive? Does he know enough, *himself*, about advertising? And if he doesn't, does it matter?'

My own view is that it does matter. Clients today, no less than yesterday, are looking – at least at times – for a *man* (not a group) who has (to quote Jim Young) 'the knowledge, skills, experience and insights to advise advertisers on how to use advertising to accomplish their objectives.'

I'm not advocating the return of the one-man-band, nor the invariable use of the first person singular. I am suggesting that more of us ought to know more than we do; and that anyone entrusted with an account should be able to give, personally, expert advice to his client without having to say: 'I'll call a group meeting tomorrow morning and let you have our thoughts as soon as possible.' Could this just possibly be why more and more clients want to talk directly to the creative people?

So the first thing Jim Young didn't say was: 'Staff an account with an account group, which is a collection of specialists under the supervision of a man who isn't one himself.' If he had felt that, he wouldn't have given the book the title he did.

Many of you will know that Young, for years, used to write a series of book reviews for the New York office house magazine. And his constant sub-heading for these reviews was: 'The best books about advertising are not about advertising' – because Young believed that the really good Advertising Man should not only know a great deal about all aspects of advertising, but also a great deal about the real world outside. In his book he says this: 'No limits can be placed on the kinds of knowledge that are useful to the Advertising Man. Indeed, it can safely be said that the broader his education, and the better stocked his mental pantry, the better at his job he is likely to be.' And he goes on: 'Every really good creative person in advertising whom I have known has always had two noticeable characteristics. First, there was no subject under the sun in which he could not easily get interested. Second, he was an extensive browser in all sorts of fields.'

As I look at the advertising being produced at the moment, at least in Britain, it seems to me that much of it has been produced in total isolation from the real world. The prose style that's used in press copy owes nothing to any other prose style except that used in other advertisements. The makers of advertisements seem increasingly obsessed by only one subject: advertisements. If this is so, then two consequences will follow. First, since the receivers of advertisements are only too conscious of the rest of the world – socially, politically, culturally, economically – then the advertisement will fail adequately to connect the advertised brand or service to that bigger, truer world. And second, imitation and lack of originality become more likely. Advertising is feeding, I think, far too much on advertising, and not nearly enough on the wider, far more interesting world outside. We are becoming a bit like those economic forecasters who refuse to study, let alone build into their forecasts, social trends and human emotions.

Sometimes today we say about another: 'He's the complete advertising professional' – by which we mean he lives, eats and sleeps nothing but advertising and his clients' problems. He reads nothing but advertisements, talks nothing but advertising, plays nothing but golf with the advertising manager.

What Jim Young didn't say was that he would regard such a man not as a professional but as a narrow-minded amateur. *His* true professional was 'an extensive browser in all sorts of fields' – social, political and cultural. Movies, television, novels good and bad, biographies, specialist magazines in which he isn't personally interested, gossip, newspapers national and local: Jim Young's professional knows them all – and relates them all back to the job he does.

Isn't it just possible that we, today, tend to think of Young's professional as a dilettante? And isn't it just possible that our clients, obsessed as they have to be with labour relations, government intervention and the price and availability of cocoa beans and packaging material, might not welcome an advertising adviser with a wider knowledge and a wider view of the world than they themselves have the time or the inclination to acquire?

Let me turn now to Chapter IV, entitled 'Knowledge of Propositions'.

Says Young: 'Before you ever put pen to paper to prepare the advertisement, script or storyboard, you had better:

1. Be crystal clear in your own mind what the proposition is.

2. Have reason to believe that it is an appealing proposition to the particular group of people you are addressing.'

We all have some doubts today about the word 'proposition' because it seems to imply input rather than response. (See *The consumer has a mind as well as a stomach*, page 115.) I'm fairly certain, and this is a presumptuous statement, that Jim Young himself would happily agree that it is more useful, or less dangerous, to think in terms of consumer response, rather than messages or propositions; if only because there's a great deal of internal evidence in his book to suggest that's the way he instinctively thought. He took response theory so much for granted that he hardly bothers to stress its importance.

Just one example to justify this bold assertion. On the subject of messages he makes the point that simply gaining attention is not enough. What you must do, says Young, is 'say something which, in effect, makes him say: "Hello, what's this?" What you must say is something carefully calculated to touch an exposed nerve of your prospect's self-interest.'

And he quotes two headlines which he once ran as a comparative test in mailorder bookselling:

'The Principles of Accounting by J.C.Bentley'

'Are you an Accountant, or only a Bookkeeper?'

– and he asks the reader which produced the more orders. He doesn't actually give the answer because he doesn't have to. The second headline is not, of course, a message or a proposition; it is a very simple stimulus that provoked a very powerful response. As Young again says, 'You must make so clear the relationship between what you have to offer and the prospect's wants, needs or existing desires that, hopefully, he will say: "That's for me!"' In other words, *response*.

Therefore, I think it fair to say that strongly implicit in Young's work is Response Theory – so let me go back to his propositions:

'1. Be crystal clear in your own mind what your proposition is.

2. Have reason to believe that it is an appealing proposition to the particular group of people you are addressing.'

Now – even accepting the implicit assumption of response rather than input here – I'm not sure that we would or should accept that completely today.

I'm reminded of the producer who is alleged to have said to a new-wave film director in some exasperation: 'You mean you don't accept that a good movie should have a beginning and a middle and an end?' To which, you may remember, the director replied: 'Oh I do, I do. But not necessarily in that order.'

Young's two points remain almost self-evidently valid: but not necessarily in that order. As we use qualitative interviews and group discussions more and more to get insights into the minds of our markets, we quite frequently discover what our proposition should be (Point 1) only *after* we've found out a great deal about the particular group of people we are addressing (Point 2).

In reality, the process is probably semi-circular anyway: you may start with Point 2, go back to Point 1 in order to form a hypothesis, return to Point 2 to validate or invalidate – and so on. Whatever the sequence, the objective must be right: as Young says later, 'I hope it will be clear to you how close is the relationship between the definition of your Proposition and the definition of your Market.'

Throughout the book, Young uses the word 'market' in a consistent and very specific sense. Not in the way that we talk about the beer market or the paper towel market or the wet soup market – but as a target group: a phrase I've never had much confidence in at the best of times.

Long before people became openly doubtful about the value of standard demographics and started talking about psychographics, Young had this to say: 'Often the key denominator of what constitutes a market is some *qualitative* factor of taste, interest or habit, not always indicated by the more measurable factors of income, age, education, home-ownership, etc. and not registered in available statistics.'

This seems to me just as true now as it ever was. The habit of defining a market, or a target group, as 'C1, C2 housewives, 25–34, with children' seems just as pointless and unhelpful. Unless you know why your market is your market, you won't find it easy either to understand them or to appeal to them.

It's often said of the J. Walter Thompson London office that the only time we show evidence of real imagination and originality is when we design leaving cards. According to the myth, this is because creativity is unshackled as the creative people are freed from the deadening effect of strategies, account planners, account executives and clients. If it *is* true, and if there *is* a reason, I suspect it's quite a different reason and almost the opposite of the myth. The writers and designers of the leaving card do not have unlimited freedom: they have very limited freedom indeed. They have to produce a leaving card that is precisely right for one particular individual. Their good fortune is that they know that one individual very well indeed. If you asked anyone to write and design a leaving card for an A/B 25–34 male living in the South East of England, married with 2.4 children, I doubt you'd get the customary degree of relevance and originality.

Still on the subject of markets, Young has another point to make, one that I believe to be vastly more important today than ever.

We are all aware of the problem of what tends to be called 'advertising clutter'. We are bombarded with statistics that demonstrate that the average US housewife is subjected to 16.6 million commercial messages every day before lunch. We use phrases like 'share of mind' (which doesn't seem to me to mean anything very much). At least in part because of all this research, particularly in the United States at the moment, there is considerable dependence on a research system that Jim Young never heard about, called Day-After-Recall.

The day after a commercial has been screened, Mrs Burke's telephonists get to work and they phone around until they've talked to a given number of people who claim to have been watching the programme in which the commercial was placed. On the basis of these people's answers to certain questions, and for a considerable fee, Mrs Burke will then tell you whether your commercial beat, or did not beat, the 'norm' for that category. So if the norm is 24 and you get 29 you're still in business, but if you get 19 you're in trouble.

One of the questions Mrs Burke and her competitors *don't* ask is whether the people answering the telephone were likely to be in the market (in Jim Young's sense) in the first place.

Yet, as Young has said, 'People select the advertisements they will give attention to just as they select the news items they will read in a newspaper. They can make an immediate classification of both as: "Of Interest" or "Not of Interest". They will classify your advertisement as "Of Interest" in proportion as they are "in the market" for what you have to offer them.'

The only way, now as then, to gain and *hold* attention is to evoke the response, 'That's for me.'

To quote Young: 'Few, if any, products or propositions have universal appeal at a given moment in time.'

So if our market is ten per cent of the population, of which half isn't watching that particular television programme, Mrs Burke's telephonists are very expensively telling us whether or not our commercial was remembered by the 95 per cent of people we didn't want to influence in the first place.

Let me move now to what I find perhaps the most valuable part of Jim Young's book: Chapter IX, 'How Advertising Works'. He says: 'We can discern, I think, that there are five basic ways in which advertising works. These are:
1. By *familiarising* – that is, as the dictionary says, by "making something well-known; bringing into common use". We will

see that this is the absolutely basic value created by advertising, the one underlying all others.

2. By *reminding* – a function that may alone, in some cases, make advertising pay.

3. By *spreading news* – not only news in the newspaper sense, but a special kind of news that only advertising, in the commercial field, can most widely deal with.

4. By *overcoming inertias* – the great drag on all human progress, economic or non-economic, as represented in the sociological term, "cultural lag".

5. By *adding a value not in the product* – the most challenging field for creativeness in advertising.'

And I'd like to take those five basic functions and examine them – re-examine them – one by one.

First: by *familiarising*. The more I think about this one, the more I agree with Jim Young that it is the 'absolutely basic value created by advertising, the one underlying all others'; and the more I believe that it is also the one we may have forgotten most about.

The whole phenomenon of *fame* is one I believe we would do well to examine; I'm not aware that anyone's done it properly. Why do people want to be famous? Why do people who aren't famous and never will be, want other people to be famous? Why do people collect autographs? Why are signed copies of books more valuable then unsigned copies? Why will I somehow manage to get into the conversation the fact that my son's friend's father once flew the Atlantic in the next seat to Greta Garbo? Why are famous objects (brands, products) more valuable than unknown ones?

Some of the answers to these questions can seem apparently rational: rarity value, collectors' items, guarantee of quality. But in fact, these aren't really answers at all: they just lead to further questions. Why is rarity a value? Why do collectors want to collect it? – and so on.

But let us all accept for the moment that Young is right: and that the familiar or the famous person or object *does* have an extra value. Common sense, observation, self-examination, gossip columns, fan clubs all suggest beyond much argument that fame is valuable.

Clearly, the implications for advertising and advertisers are very considerable. Simply *being known* is worth something – often a great deal.

The first implication for us and our clients is that to advertise at all – *almost irrespective of content* – is worthwhile. And the penalties of *not* advertising can be considerable.

Take Adidas. Adidas is famous. It hasn't done much conventional advertising but it's made certain that everyone in its market knows it exists, and what it's associated with. People pay extra for Adidas bags *because* they've got the name on, *because* it's famous – so making them even more famous. Fame equals value.

Fame doesn't have to be based on quality or aptitude: it can be self-generated. The Queen, our Queen, is famous for being famous – and would be even if she was a rotten Queen. Newsreaders and weather-forecasters become famous not because of their skill in reading other people's words from an autocue, but through familiarity. And, for no other reason, they are then offered quite large sums of money to open supermarkets. Fame has a value.

We all know that, over the last seven years, the average sum of advertising money being spent by the average manufacturer of branded goods has declined significantly in real terms. We all know the reasons for this and I don't propose to go over them again. What I would like to do is suggest an additional reason.

More and more, agencies compete among themselves on the basis of advertising *content.* Often, the sum of money the client proposes to spend is predetermined; so in a competitive pitch, each agency is in effect trying to convince the prospective client that it can spend the given, say, $1 million more effectively than any other agency. Few, if any, dare suggest that the $1 million should be $2 million: it might sound as if the proposing agency needed twice as much money as its competitors to achieve the same result.

Over the years, therefore, there has been a concerted, continued, almost orchestrated emphasis on content (or 'creativity') and virtually *no* emphasis on the virtues of advertising *at all* at a weight that will make a brand famous or maintain a brand's existing fame.

And it seems to me that by reminding ourselves and our clients of this 'absolutely basic value', without shame and without being scared of any accusations of self-interest, we could be giving them the advice they need even more desperately than 'improved creativity' – whatever that might mean.

A brand that isn't famous isn't a brand – it's a product. A famous brand enjoys an extra value, can command a reasonable price from retailer and consumer and can therefore deliver a more respectable margin. Have we forgotten? And have we let our clients forget as well?

Second: 'By *reminding* – a function that may alone, in some cases, make advertising pay.' Here, Jim Young makes it clear that he's using the word in its original sense of reminding: jogging a memory that may have forgotten.

Advertising may remind us that St. Valentine's Day is coming up, or Mother's Day, or Hallowe'en. Or it may remind us of the satisfactions of a product once enjoyed but allowed to slip off our mental repertoire of purchases. Or it may remind us that a particular time of day, or a particular occasion, are particularly suitable for the consumption of a particular product.

Advertising that tells us Product X is the Anytime Drink is not going to remind us of anything. But if it reminds us that it's the Sunday lunch drink or the bedtime drink or the convalescent drink, then those times and those occasions may themselves later trigger off the thought of the product.

The third of Jim Young's functions: 'By *spreading news* – not only news in the newspaper sense, but a special kind of news that only advertising, in the commercial field, can most widely deal with.' Here, Jim Young is making the important distinction between what he calls 'newspaper-type' news – news which happens anyway – and news which is *created* by the Advertising Man.

Clearly, the launch of a new car, the development of a low calorie soft drink, next week's low prices in a chain of supermarkets, a Christmas sale – all these are news and will, or should, be featured in the advertising.

It is by drawing our attention to the other kind of news, the kind that has to be created, that Young helps us most. To quote him again: 'The vitality which news gives to advertising is so great, that when it is not available built-in, no Advertising Man will fail to seek it elsewhere.'

Which means that we – Jim Young's ideal Advertising Men – should instigate new product improvements (why don't you put a handle on the Kodak Instamatic?); should suggest new uses for existing products (why don't we advertise Johnson's baby products for grown-up ladies?). The invention of new recipes is news creation – and news, what's more, that's unlike newspaper news, that is designed as Jim Young says 'to persuade people to do something'.

The ability to make news, to turn old facts into new news, to relate to ever changing external events, I'm sure should be one of the skills of the Advertising Man; which in turn relates to the point made earlier that *only* if we're aware of the activities of the proper world outside *can* we relate them back to our clients' products.

Jim Young's fourth function: 'By *overcoming inertias*: the great drag on all human progress.' In Chapter XIII, Jim Young says: 'No matter how effective an advertisement may be in creating interest and desire, there is always some loss in response due to the inertia which keeps people from taking even the action they might have been disposed to take.'

Take selling insurance and selling tyres as two extreme examples of the problem of overcoming inertia. Everybody knows, probably, that they *could* be better insured, that they *should* buy new tyres. But, as Jim Young says, 'There are common causes for the inertia in all such cases: either the reward for action is remote and often intangible; or the penalty for inaction is delayed. What kind of advertising message has a chance to overcome such inertia? Only one that will arouse such fear of the delayed penalty, or such a vivid vision of the remote reward, that the emotional reaction will burn out the inertial block to action.'

Social advertising – seat-belts, drug abuse, drinking and driving, anti-smoking – in many countries provides good examples of 'arousing fears of the delayed penalty'.

If it is true, as Jim Young suggests, that 'inertia is, in some degree, a constant in the advertising equation', do we, I wonder, consciously think deeply enough about the problem of overcoming it? Of getting an *immediate response*?

Retailers and mail-order companies tend not to forget: 'Limited Edition!', 'Hurry while stocks last!', 'Offer closes 16 July!', 'This week only!', 'Order before 25 October and you'll get a FREE plastic toothpick!' We can learn from them.

And then Jim Young's fifth function: 'By *adding a value not in the product* – the most challenging field for creativeness in advertising.' I'm sometimes told that while we all recognise this as an important function of advertising, of building a brand, we really shouldn't talk about it aloud because it plays into the hands of consumerists, price commissions and government regulatory agencies who want to prove that we're selling fantasies not realities – and charging more for them.

I have to say that I find this a cowardly and slightly dishonest attitude.

As Jim Young says, 'subjective values are no less real than tangible ones. Nobody has ever criticised the advertising which has made Steinway "The Instrument of Immortals" and given added pride to every owner of one.'

And that's the point. *If* the product delivers functionally and *if* subjective values are added, then the user or buyer has got his or her money's worth and will thank you for it.

If we're not prepared to argue that point out to the consumerists, the price commissions and the regulatory agencies, then we shouldn't be doing it. The truth, of course, is that – whether advertising exists or not – people add subjective values to alternative products themselves. They always have and they always will.

Young says: 'This use of advertising – to add a subjective value to the product – becomes increasingly important as the trends in our technology lead to competing products becoming more and more alike.'

We know that's more true than ever. We tell our clients that it's more true than ever. We are, at our best, quite good at doing it. It can enable our clients to build businesses and make respectable profits. It gives consumers more choice and more satisfaction. Why, I wonder, should we be shy of talking about it?

So those are Jim Young's five functions for advertising – except for one point which he makes right at the beginning and which I have deliberately left for the end. After initially itemising the five different functions, he says: 'It should be said at once that, whereas some advertising may soundly be devoted to one of these uses alone; and in nearly all advertising one of them will be primary; *most advertising will involve two or more of these uses.*'

So, of course, we do not have to choose between one or four or three or five. The main value of these five categories is to make us answer that critical question: 'What is this advertising trying to achieve?' and also: 'Which role is the primary role?'

And finally, another comment on what Jim Young *didn't* say. Not because he was ignorant or unenlightened but because in his time it didn't need to be said. Let me return to the word 'creativity'. It seems to me that today, in many countries, advertising agencies are evaluated primarily on what is called creativity – and such research as has been done bears out this view. There seems to be a single scale, a single dimension, like this:

Dull		Visible
Old-fashioned		Fashionable
←	————————————————	→
No awards		Awards

The nearer you are to the left of this scale, the worse you are; and the nearer to the right, the better you are. And this perception of agencies – what might be termed the Clio Effect – seems to be held by clients, potential clients, trade press journalists, suppliers, and perhaps most strongly of all by the people who work in agencies.

What Jim Young didn't say – because he didn't have to – was that this was not his perception of agencies at all. He clearly had at the back – and the front – of his mind, a rather different dimension: a different scale altogether.

Two scales this time, with the upright line a dotted line: to suggest, as I believe, that it has lost its value. At the top: 'It works. Responsive. Advertis*ing*.' And at the bottom: 'Irresponsible. Self-indulgent. Advertis*ements*.' (To which one might add: ignorant, amateur, thoughtless.)

Increasingly, advertising is talked about as though it had no function. We ourselves refer to our 'creative product' as though the advertisements we produce were ends in themselves, to be looked at and evaluated as if they were pictures in an art gallery.

In Jim Young's book, the word 'creativity' is used very infrequently; and when he does use it, he uses it virtually as a synonym for effectiveness.

There are two ways of judging the Sydney Opera House. First: what does it *look* like? Is it aesthetically pleasing? Is it original and imaginative as a piece of design, as a piece of architecture? Second: does it *work*? Does it function as an opera house? Are the auditoriums the right size? Can you park? Is there enough height over the stage for storing scenery? Is it acoustically satisfactory?

More and more, when we look at our own work, we ask only the first set of questions. What does it look like on our showreel? Will it be a good advertisement for us? Will it make us seem 'creative'? When we should, of course, be asking: did it work? Did it make the client more successful? How did it do it?

I believe Jim Young would be, if not horrified, certainly bewildered.

I'm not suggesting that the horizontal line is unimportant nor that it will go away. I am suggesting that it is our job, as managers, to reinstate that vertical line in the minds of all those who evaluate advertising and advertising agencies.

'Did it work?' If it did, then it was – in the proper sense – creative. It created a desire in the mind of the market. It was money well spent. It is why advertising exists.

The horizontal line doesn't need to be argued: either an advertisement seems to be inventive and original or it doesn't. That's all you can say as a judge or a potential client viewing a showreel.

The vertical scale, effectiveness, is by contrast invisible. It's one of the biggest mistakes in the business to believe the old saying, 'Good advertising speaks for itself.' It doesn't. Somebody – us – has to speak for it. Somebody has to say: 'This was the problem, this was the budget, this was the competition, this is what the market thought, this is what they wanted to hear, this is how we thought of saying it, this is how we changed and improved it, this is the finished result – and this is what happened to sales.'

If you wanted to plot J. Walter Thompson on the map, I know where I'd like us to be – in the top, right-hand corner, as near to the top of the vertical scale as possible – and as near to the right of the horizontal scale as possible. But in that order.

Some of the accounts we handle, because of their nature and their consumers, allow us to develop – indeed, they demand – self-evidently 'creative' campaigns. Not one of those opportunities should be lost: our clients need them and so do we. But some of the accounts we handle do *not* necessarily require self-evidently creative treatment – and we're being irresponsible when we try to make them that way.

Every account ought to be high on the vertical scale. Every account should have a good story to tell, even if not an award-winning commercial to show.

I have been told on occasions that, in today's world, this approach sounds defensive and apologetic; that to talk about effectiveness sounds like an excuse for not being creative. I don't believe it. What, after all, are clients *paying for*?

We can't go on playing a game when we secretly disapprove of the rules.

Let's go back to James Webb Young: 'The true Advertising Man, as the term is used in this book, is he who has the knowledge, skills, experience and insights to advise advertisers how best to use advertising to accomplish their objectives.'

'*Accomplish* their *objectives*': that is the key phrase.

It was suggested yesterday that agency people had to choose between being a creative person and being a businessman. The last thing Jim Young didn't say was that he would not have accepted the need to make such a distinction – and neither do I.

Consumer identification: the PG Chimps and the novelist's mother

Marketing, March 1996

The reason why so many television commercials are stuffed with so many boring people is because of a theory called consumer identification.

The theory goes like this: if you want to get millions of very ordinary C2 people to buy your brand, you must cast your commercial with very ordinary C2-looking people. Those watching will then respond thus: 'Aha! I see that this brand is used by very ordinary C2 persons not unlike myself. I will therefore from henceforth buy this brand and no other.'

As a theory, it's flawed for several hundred reasons but I will concentrate on two; the first being best illustrated by the case of the novelist's mother.

He was a good friend and had just written his first novel which was transparently autobiographical. His mother was a perfectly frightful woman and in his book he had portrayed her with an accuracy made effortless by 23 years of closely observed loathing. It was only as the book was published that he began to worry – but there was little he could do. So he inscribed a copy with some well-fashioned insincerity, sent it off to her and waited. A week or two later they met.

'Darling,' she said. 'What perfectly frightful people you do seem to know.'

That's the first flaw: people don't identify with people like themselves.

When I come across holiday advertisements featuring late middle-aged gentlemen with wispy white hair in cardigans and garden chairs, I am often in a cardigan and a garden chair myself. I know exactly what I am supposed to do: I am supposed to identify. In fact what I do is distance. I can't be the only person who doesn't want to go on holiday to meet people like myself.

Predicaments and problems, ambitions and emotions: that's what people identify with. You don't have to be black to identify with Othello: just jealous.

The second flaw is to think that the function of people in advertisements is to define the brand's users. It is not. It is to define the brand. And that's what they'll do whether you mean them to or not.

I do not know how many people there are in Great Britain who talk, dress, and entertain as people in After Eight commercials talk, dress and entertain. I do know that there aren't enough of them to eat 127 tons of After Eight every week.

One of the many reasons for the longevity and success of the PG chimps is that they portray reality, reassuringly, at one remove. Transpose in your mind all those chimp people back into real people and you've got a series of patronising situations with which nobody would have identified and which would have plunged the brand irreversibly down-market.

Clients and casting directors form an unholy alliance. They want ordinary people – but not too ordinary, you understand. So they choose people with no personality but preternaturally clean finger-nails.

Perhaps it's only people who earn their living portraying ordinary people in commercials who really do identify with the people they see in commercials. But then, as we know from the case of the novelist's mother, that doesn't happen either.

Avoid criticism: write ads that nobody reads

Marketing, August 1997

Much bad advertising is bad not because it's off strategy or unpersuasive but because it's invisible. Absolutely nobody sees it, and so it represents the ultimate in waste.

This is the sort of advertising that should be regularly and publicly roasted yet very seldom is. And the reason, of course, is that it's invisible. Nobody roasts it because nobody reads it.

I may be the only person in the world to have read and noted the following copy:

'In every era, the few who make the difference are those who dare to imagine a world beyond the horizon. A world in which old truths are enriched with new ones. The greater the resources, the greater the possibilities.'

Superimposed on this gibberish are two much bigger words at right-angles to each other. One is OBLITERATE and the other OBSTACLES. If you look very closely indeed, you will notice that a vertical rule in the left margin is in fact a legend listing the number of employees, offices and billions of dollars of assets that the bank in question can boast.

Yes, as you will already have guessed, this work is for a bank. And since I'm the only person to have read it, it falls to me to roast it.

I've no idea which language this advertisement was translated from or even which language it has been translated into. But as it happens, it doesn't matter. And it doesn't matter because – even had the words made sense and expressed something of interest to the reader – *nobody could ever have read them.*

The words above appear not in a newspaper but on one of those illuminated panels in international airports. Reasonably so, you might think: you are an international investment bank; your audience is international; international people may be expected to use international airports.

But these displays are on the walls of walkways. People walk along them. Being international business people to whom time is money, they walk along them briskly. Quite often there are moving belts, along which people also walk briskly. Even for the curious and the preternaturally keen-sighted, maximum reading time available is four seconds, or two if you're on the moving belt.

I cannot believe that this bank would spend money on any other purchase with such a total lack of common sense. Several people in the bank must have read the words; were they too embarrassed to ask what they meant? Somebody must have authorised the acquisition of the illuminated panels; did it not occur to them to ask how a busy person moving at ten miles an hour could be expected to read and absorb 40 words of gobbledegook from a distance of several feet?

The clients themselves must be international business people. They must be exposed to their own advertisements many times a day in many cities. How can they let them survive?

Or is it, perhaps, that they've just never seen them?

The new Stella Artois:
unnvervingly inexpensive

Marketing, February 1997

I've always believed that 'reassuringly expensive' was one of the great positioning statements of our time. Now a promotional twelve-pack (to which I shall return) has made me try to work out why. It's been a brain-damaging business, as you'll soon see.

With the exception of Stella (and the occasional dismissive reference to a competitor) the words cheap and expensive are never used in advertising. Critics believe this is because copywriters are a slimy lot who can't bring themselves to be straight about anything, but for once that's not true. The reason the words aren't used is because none of us much wants to buy either cheap things or expensive things. Nor, even, do we want to buy middle-priced things. What we want is good things at the 'right' price. This simple concept used to be called value; but value has now been so thoroughly debased through its use as a euphemism for cheap that we need something else. Language, like money, is a currency extremely susceptible to inflation.

What we want is for things to be worth it: worth the money, worth the price. And worth is made up of satisfaction – which is subjective – at an acceptable pain threshold of price.

This, of course, does not mean that the lower the price the higher the satisfaction because we don't always know how to judge worth. Estimating worth involves making competitive judgments about elusive concepts such as quality. So, confusingly, (are you still with me?) we look to price to help us. Price has to be both low and high; but not too low or the possibility of worth becomes improbable; and not too high or the satisfaction snaps.

Furthermore, what you think is good is different from what I think is good; and what I think is expensive you regard as dead reasonable. When advertisements tell me that the object on offer costs less than I think, I become enraged. How can they know how much I think it costs when I do not know myself how much I think it costs and they decline to tell me?

I hope this has clarified things a bit. What it means is that most advertising for above-market-price items is trying to raise belief in (and perhaps even contribute to the delivery of) worth, to the point where the price, when finally revealed, meets both requirements: low enough to be acceptable and high enough to act as confirmation of quality.

And that, of course, (which you knew all along) is why 'reassuringly expensive' is so brilliant.

Somebody, however, seems to have forgotten. There's this promotional pack of Stella Artois in the off-trade at the moment – 12 for the price of 10 – and the legend on it says: 'Reassuringly Good Value.'

I hope for the long-term prosperity of the brand that I'm the only person to have noticed it. And I certainly wouldn't dream of passing it on.

High noon at Elkhart, Indiana

The drive for new business obsesses agencies. New business presentations combine tension, expense and absurdity in roughly equal proportions. This one happened in the 1960s but I didn't write about it until 1987, when the following article appeared in *Campaign.*

Unwisely, as it turned out, I told one or two people what I was going to do before I went. 'There's this very important new business presentation in Elkhart, Indiana,' I said. 'Six of us will be going down from New York on Wednesday. Henry, Tom, three or four others from the New York office – and me, representing The World.'

Henry was President and Tom was International Director. I'd never been asked to represent The World before and was naturally gratified. As it turned out, The World was all those bits that weren't the United States but that still left quite a lot.

I'd been told we'd be rehearsing for most of the Tuesday in New York. We had a lot to cover and only a couple of hours for the presentation. Rehearsal was essential. It was going to be slick and seamless. A great many millions of dollars were at stake worldwide.

I flew to New York with a 16mm reel of commercials (in those days, they could only show 16mm in Elkhart, Indiana). It was very cold indeed when I walked to the office at 8 am on Tuesday morning and I was glad of my new overcoat. I went first to Tom's office. He was in a meeting. So was Henry. And so were Kevin, Bob and Bill. They were all in different meetings, but were planning to meet mid-afternoon at La Guardia. We were to fly to Chicago, then to South Bend where we would spend the night. We would rehearse there before going on to Elkhart the following morning.

I went out to La Guardia with Tom, who was going to write his bit on the plane. It had been a very hectic week. For the first time we all met and Kevin, who was in charge of administration, handed out the tickets. There was a ticket for everyone but The World, so I went off and bought one for myself. Outside it started to snow.

We were the last commercial flight to be allowed to land at O'Hare that day. We had to wait an hour while they chipped the snow away from the gate before we could get off. The connecting flight to South Bend had been cancelled so we checked into the Ramada Inn. Outside it was still snowing and getting colder.

We had dinner and much imported burgundy in the baronial dining room, where the waiters wore wigs and knee-breeches and there was a dance band. The band-leader's wife was very decorative and Henry, who looked not unlike Cary Grant, asked her to dance. The band-leader went on leading the band but with his head facing the dance floor. I'd never seen that before.

At 1 am we had a final stinger and started to go to bed. When I told the receptionist that my new overcoat had been stolen from the cloakroom, he very kindly gave me a raincoat instead. Its hem stopped just short of my shoes, it was stained all the way down the front and it had no buttons. The receptionist also apologised for the absence of water: the mains supply had frozen.

As I was getting into bed, the phone rang. Henry had booked rooms for the two of us at The Flying Carpet, where they had water. The taxi was waiting. I got dressed, put on the raincoat and joined Henry, leaving my watch on the bedside console.

Soon after 2 am we checked into The Flying Carpet Motel and Henry discovered the piano bar. We ordered stingers and Henry got into conversation with three lawyers. One had made an air hostess pregnant, one had been caught importing yen illegally into Canada and the third was drinking along with the other two out of sympathy. Henry, not a lawyer and knowing nothing of tax, began giving them advice on tax law. Impressed, they began calling him sir and buying him stingers. He was still accepting them graciously when I went to bed again at 3.30 am.

On Wednesday morning, I phoned Bob at the Ramada Inn to ask if he could find my watch. He, Tom, Kevin and Bill had already spent an hour trying to find Henry and me. Henry hadn't told them we had moved. In the airport bus Henry told me that, in his experience, after a certain hour it was better not to go to bed at all. He then fell silent.

We took off for South Bend in a gentle blizzard and Tom returned to his speech. It was exactly the time we should have been starting our presentation in Elkhart, Indiana, but Kevin had called the client to explain.

After 20 minutes, the chief stewardess brought us all up to date with the news. The airport at South Bend had closed. Normally we would be returning to Chicago. However, our pilot hadn't obtained the necessary qualifications for landing that type of aircraft in the conditions then prevailing at O'Hare, so instead we'd be landing at Fort Wayne, where conditions were much the same.

We were the last commercial flight to be allowed to land at Fort Wayne that day. Henry sat in a corner with his eyes shut and Kevin went to call the client. Tom went through his notes, lips moving slightly as he did so.

Kevin came back with the news that the client was sending the company QueenAir to fetch us. It could fly under the weather at 800 feet.

Henry opened his eyes and told us that he was to begin a vacation in Jamaica the following day and would wait at Fort Wayne until the first proper aircraft left for anywhere. He would not be going to Elkhart. The QueenAir slithered in.

There were five of us and four seats so Kevin sat on the lavatory at the back.

We arrived at Elkhart, Indiana, were issued with security badges, walked through the factory and were shown into the meeting room.

The ashtrays were full, the projector was unmanned, there were no windows and no clients. We were seven hours late.

Bill put his slide tray on the carousel. He was going to tell them how he had co-ordinated Pepsi-Cola advertising in Latin America. I fed my reel into the projector.

Two clients came in. Bob and Kevin, who had met them before, introduced me as coming from England. One client, beyond surprise, nodded and said: 'England'. He'd heard of it.

Tom, leader in Henry's absence, started. He bent his head and read slowly from his reminder cards. 'At J. Walter Thompson,' he read, 'we are international, resourceful.' Here he stopped, having reached the bottom of his first card.

After only a moment's hesitation he realised that he should turn over to the next, which he managed at the first attempt. His head bent lower. 'And dynamic,' he said doubtfully.

Bill had reached Chile when the first client left the room to make a telephone call. As Bill finished, the second and last client left the room without explanation. It was my turn.

Tom looked at his watch and then at me. 'I think you'd better start anyway,' he said.

For 12 minutes, I spoke about The World to Tom, Bill, Bob and Kevin.

They looked at me loyally and nodded from time to time. One client returned when I was showing an After Eight commercial. The second never returned.

Tom asked if the client had any questions. The client said: 'Are you hoping to get back to Chicago tonight?'

As I picked up the raincoat, Tom said: 'Your suit's split down the back.' It had.

Back at work in London the following Monday, I got into the lift. 'How did it go?' they asked.

4
Making advertising happen

Training creative people to carry newspapers

International Journal of Advertising, 1990

A long time ago, long before she became Maureen Lipman, Joyce Grenfell was half-way through her one-woman show to a packed and appreciative audience at the Fortune Theatre. The reviews had been excellent and, on her own admission, she was pretty pleased with herself. Then, in the middle of a dramatic silence she was rightly proud of being able to sustain, she heard a clear, ten-year-old voice from the stalls.

'Mummy,' it said. 'What is that lady for?'

As a question, it enjoys a certain healthy fundamentalism, which is why it's always a good one to ask: about governments, trade associations, laws, companies, conferences – and creative people in advertising agencies. What are they all *for*?

It should be very easy indeed to say what creative people are for – indeed, I think it is – but it seldom gets spelt out explicitly. I don't remember ever being told what my job really was: it was left to me to find out for myself. And while that kind of journey of self-discovery may be very good for the moral fibre, it can be a confusing and demoralising experience.

One obvious way of deducing what's expected of you is to work at it empirically. You register the times when you're praised and the times when you're shouted at; make a note of which caused what; and then attempt to incur more of the former and less of the latter. This is how dogs learn to carry newspapers.

So when your creative director goes out of his way to congratulate you on some new work, you know that the essence of your job is to earn the approval of your creative director. After all, he must know good advertising when he sees it: that's what he's paid all that money for.

Later that day, the same piece of work is rejected with contempt by the client. That in itself may not be too disconcerting; it's well known that clients are poor judges of advertising which is why they need agencies. It gets more perplexing when the client (who is a poor judge of advertising) embraces your campaign with enthusiasm while your creative director (who knows good advertising when he sees it) comes back from holiday and stamps all over it.

Then there is the client who awards the agency a huge new account entirely on the strength of your creative work. Is he still a poor judge of advertising? If so, is it ethical to accept the account? Or perhaps clients are poor judges of advertising only when they reject work? Perhaps a client who accepts your creative work is, by definition, a good judge of advertising; except, it would seem, on those occasions when your creative director doesn't agree with him?

Your account executive may not help. 'Thanks entirely to your creative work,' she says, 'that was a great meeting. Come and have a drink.' So you wonder if your reason for existence is to produce the kind of work which makes meetings good. People praise you a lot for that.

Ten days later, the same work is sunk irrecoverably by research. And while it's well known that had people listened to research, none of the world's ten greatest campaigns would ever have seen the light of day, this particular client is inclined to listen to research, and so, by coincidence, is the account director.

So perhaps what you're for is to produce campaigns that do well in research? I knew one very respected creative person in the States whose only skill lay in 'beating the norms', as he put it. Work that does well in research has a much better chance of being published than work that does not. But next time you go for a job interview, and you include on your reel a lot of work that has done very well in research, the creative director of the most exciting agency in town tells you that what you're doing is aesthetically and morally indefensible.

Nor does the confusion end there. A thoroughly crafted print campaign puts up sales by 12 per cent in a declining market and your creative director doesn't even short-list it for his in-house awards. At the same time, several heavy golden objects are bestowed on a television campaign which is well known to have sold nothing to anybody and which will be withdrawn as soon as decency allows. The author of the television campaign receives a bigger merit bonus than the author of the thoroughly crafted print campaign. That year, not a single IPA Advertising Effectiveness Award goes to a piece of work that has also been recognised creatively. What on earth is going on here?

All this makes it very hard indeed for creative people to work out for themselves what they're for. So many conflicting and contradictory signals; so many different people making disconnected judgments; so many sets of rules and so many changes to each of them; the very same action incurring both gratitude and reproach – but not invariably so. If all this happened to dogs, they'd never learn to carry newspapers. As Pavlov's did, they'd go mad.

It seems to me, therefore, that much the most important first step in encouraging creative people to produce their best is to minimise confusion of purpose and inconsistency of judgment. We need to be a bit more explicit about what creative people are for and to make sure that the view is understood and shared.

We know what media buyers are for. Media buyers are for buying time and space. So are creative people for filling the time and space the media buyers have bought? Only up to a point; and the point in question is that absolutely anyone can fill time and space. What creative people are for is to fill any given item of time or space in such a manner that the client gets a better return on the investment in that time or space than he would have done had the time or space been filled by any old person. I apologise for such a clumsy and insultingly obvious definition but I don't remember having seen it anywhere before.

The calculation goes like this. Cost of time or space: 100 units of currency. Value to client of time or space left empty: minus 100. Value to client of time or space filled by any old person: anything from nought to, say, 110. Value to client of time or space filled by (good) creative person: say, 120 – and on occasions, of course, a good deal more.

Why creative persons deserve to be called creative is not just because they can think of things that the rest of us can't. It's because they can *make things happen* in a way that the rest of us can't: more quickly or more economically or more rewardingly or more lastingly.

They can help people understand complex arguments; they can bring freshness to old promises; they can engage people's minds and self-interest; they can develop a narrative; they can forge connections through visual and verbal metaphor. And they do all these things and many more not for the sake of it but as a calculated means to a clearly understood end. They use their skills and talents and imagination in order to make certain things happen.

But do they always know which precise things they're expected to make happen? Almost as bad as not knowing what you're for is not knowing what the advertising is for. The longest and apparently most comprehensive of briefs often fails to answer that most useful of all questions: what is the advertising expected to do?

To tell them portentously that the objective of the advertising is to increase sales doesn't help creative people at all. The brighter of them might even have guessed that for themselves. What they need to know, and agree with, is: which people might respond more favourably to the brand in the future if they felt or thought about it differently? Once that's understood and agreed, all subsequent discussion and debate has at least a chance of being constructive. Creative people understandably get demotivated very quickly if comment and criticism are presented in an erratic confusion of strategy and execution.

There are, in addition, a few other rules-of-thumb for managers that are worth at least thinking about.

In the development stage of advertising, very poor first thoughts often receive far more time and tender loving care than promising ones. This is almost always the wrong way round. A lot of time and care spent on a rotten idea can sometimes make it almost adequate. Exactly the same expenditure can turn a promising campaign into a brilliant one. Being told to start again is never enjoyable, but the pain doesn't last very long and vanishes completely as soon as the new idea materialises. Having a sub-standard idea nibbled to death by ducks goes on being unpleasant for months and leaves nothing to be proud of at the end of it.

Like any other currency, praise can get debased. You are not, therefore, demonstrating your creative management skills by describing everything you see as fantastic. By the time you see something good, your opinion will be worthless.

You hope your creative people will try to understand their audience; it's well worth your while trying to understand them. Knowing you've got to think of something can make you feel very lonely and vulnerable and bad-tempered – that's one of the reasons that working in pairs is so popular among creative people. It really is a different sort of job – or should be; but that doesn't mean you have to treat them with reverence.

Above all, remind your creative people what they're for, remind them what the advertising's for, and concentrate the praise on those who deliver. They're not always the most obvious candidates.

Irresponsibility at Princeton

By 1970, I had been creative director of J. Walter Thompson London for six years. One of the continuing struggles in the creative department of an agency is between the apparently contradictory demands of responsible relevance and free-ranging originality. I say 'apparently' because there *is* no real conflict. What makes good advertising so hard to produce is the need to present the relevant in an arresting and rewarding manner. Neither alone is enough. Although I'd still not worked out what a creative director had to do (I never did) I had begun to understand that central to the job was the need to be as critical of irrelevance as of unoriginality. In August 1970, there was a J. Walter Thompson Worldwide creative directors' meeting in Princeton, New Jersey. It was, I think, the first such meeting; until then, only managers and senior account persons had been thought adult enough to exchange views across frontiers. The title I was given for my own contribution was *Creative Responsibility*. The piece is edited.

Rather than talk to the title I was given, which sounds a little ponderous and depressing, I've elected to concentrate on creative *ir*responsibility.

In other words, by trying to illustrate some of the areas where creative people (not of course *us*) can occasionally be irresponsible, I hope to illuminate what the nature of creative responsibility should be.

All good creative people are, by definition, responsible to some degree. They may not get into the office until lunchtime; they may get drunk at lunchtime; they may wear sneakers, beads and waist-length hair (unless they're ladies); but that's not the sort of responsibility, or lack of it, I think we should be concerned with. It's *professional* responsibility rather than personal, social or sartorial that obviously matters more to us today.

I think that all good creative people are professionally responsible: if only out of sheer self-interest, self-absorption or self-esteem. Because, more than any other member of an agency, the creative person *is* what he *does*: and he knows it. He'll work all weekend or all night or both; not, if we're honest, because he's driven by an obsessive desire to put his client's sales up by two per cent (though he'll certainly be delighted if he does). He's driven more, I think, by the sheer satisfaction of laying an absolutely beautiful egg (in the English sense of that phrase).

But we're not perfect; and neither are the people we work with. So let me look at one or two examples of creative irresponsibility that have, I'm told, been known to happen, just occasionally, in other agencies, many years ago.

'As long as it's not a washing-powder, packaged-food, pharmaceuticals, trade or corporate and spends at least two million, I'd be quite prepared to work on it.'

I suspect that in every agency there are accounts with a reputation for dreariness; so dreary people tend to be allocated to them. They proceed, predictably, to produce dreary advertising and this confirms us all in our belief that they were dreary accounts all along.

I suspect that one of the most important differences between the talented amateur and the talented professional is the professional's genuine eagerness to work on anything – irrespective of product field, previous advertising or the size of the budget. *And to make something where nothing was before.*

It seems to me to be both irresponsible and unprofessional for a creative man to deign to work only on the 'easy' accounts. One of the greatest satisfactions available to a creative man is to take an allegedly 'difficult' account and make something of it. (And when that happens, it's surprising just how many other people are suddenly interested in working on it, too.)

'Now at first sight, this might seem pretty ordinary. But if we shoot actually in Athens, with Mike Nichols directing, Twiggy as the housewife and music by McCartney, it could be sensational.'

Whenever you hear *that* from anyone (and whenever, indeed, you hear yourself saying it) you know that someone, somewhere has failed to have what you might call an *idea*. In more cases than not, I think, creative people get the reputation for irresponsibility because they try to use clients' money to add production values to a mediocre script or headline. We've all done it, and it's sad.

Many of the best commercials cost relatively little to make. The use of three helicopters and a transatlantic crane will never make a bad or non-existent idea into an effective advertisement, but it may just lead younger creative people to believe that that's what's expected of them; so it becomes not only expensive but dangerous.

As everyone knows, much concern is currently being expressed about the soaring costs of commercial production. The production companies are blamed; the agency producers and art directors are blamed; and the unions are blamed. While none may be entirely blameless, it seems to me that there may be one person more responsible than any other, and that's the writer who taps out: 'We open on an aerial shot of Hong Kong at dawn' – without recognising that those eleven words may cost a few thousand dollars each. Are they worth it? They may be; they may not. If not, is there a more imaginative way of achieving the equivalent effect?

'Don't confuse me with all that research. I'm creative.'

I don't think there's much of this left but there is just a little, and by no means all of it is the creative man's fault. Some research people feel they have failed as professionals if anything they say is comprehensible. So if you're not careful, a situation develops in which two crucial members of the same group, each of whom needs the help of the other, are using two totally different vocabularies – almost two languages.

If, as creative people, we don't know what the hell the other man is talking about, it's our responsibility to say so. It will do him a lot of good to have to emerge from behind his comfortable smokescreen of jargon and it will make it possible for us to make use of what he has to offer. The more the research man and the creative man share a way of thinking and talking about advertising, the better for both of them and the better for the account. The introduction of account planning has done more than anything else to reduce our communications gap.

'But over 84 per cent of women said they *wanted* whiteness.'

It is just as irresponsible to lean on research as an excuse for predictable work as it is to ignore it altogether. Quantified research, basic market research, by definition deals with – at best – the very recent past. What we should be concerned with is the future. It is no good feeding basic marketing information into your personal computer and hoping you'll get a new campaign. All you'll do is invent yesterday. The other thing, of course, is that research of this kind, even at its best, probably tells you what people say they want from *all* washing powders, *all* breads, *all* razor blades. But we're not concerned with all; we're concerned with this particular one. So it seems to me that here the creative man's responsibility is to use research information as raw material from which to construct a relevant new idea for his brand – but rarely if ever to use it unprocessed.

'Sure it's dull. But so's the product, for Chrissake.'

To my mind, the man who performed one of the greatest disservices to the business is the man who invented the phrase 'low-interest product'. By inventing it, he provided the excuse for a lot of low-interest advertising. I don't, myself, know what a low-interest product is. If you've got piles, a new treatment for haemorrhoids may be the highest-interest product on the market. If you're a woman who has to buy bread for her family, and if you want good bread, then bread is a high-interest product. I suspect that, most of the time, low-interest means of low interest to the creative person. If a product seems dull, then it's more likely to seem dull because of the advertising than because of any intrinsic dullness it supposedly possesses.

If it is genuinely, intrinsically, universally, irretrievably dull, then it doesn't deserve to sell in the first place – and it almost certainly won't.

'With a new name, new pack, new formulation, a lower price and a built-in virility agent, we could really do something with this one.'

It's clearly the creative man's responsibility to think of, and recommend, product improvements whenever he can. But nothing, understandably, infuriates a client more than the suggestion that his agency is incapable of producing effective advertising for his product *as it stands*. For a creative man to adopt this attitude is, I believe, irresponsible – and a total abdication of his most important role.

Existing products, old-established products, universal products, over-familiar products; these can nearly always be revived and revitalised by imaginative advertising – with the obvious proviso that they haven't become genuinely and functionally obsolete.

'I don't care how good the sales have been. Work like that could ruin my reputation.'

There are some people whose first instinct on being appointed to an account is to want to change everything, absolutely. Now, if they've been assigned to that account because it has become quite clear that everything should be changed absolutely, that's fine. But there are some accounts where the sales are good, the campaign seems fine and what is required above all is continuity and extension rather than change. So the responsible creative man looks with respect at what has gone before (even though the work was not his) and simply tries to make it that little bit better. It may not be as satisfying to his ego and it may not look as good when he goes for his next job interview; but it's what the account ought to get.

If, *at the same time,* he chooses to take a completely fresh look; to develop an alternative approach that can be evaluated, preferably in the market place, against the original – so much the better. But to instigate change simply because you weren't around when what exists first took shape can't be responsible. And brand managers are no less culpable than agency people in this respect.

'But I thought the client liked slice-of-life.'

Some creative people become so amazingly responsible that they become unfit for active service. It is the account man's job to know what the client likes, even if he chooses to ignore it. It is the creative man's job to know what the client should have. That may sound arrogant and unrealistic – but it's true.

The moment a creative group, at planning stage, allows itself consciously to take into account the known (or more often, supposed) prejudices and predilections of any given client, it will lose not only its own self-respect but also any value it might have had to that client.

'What d'you mean, why? I tell you it's great, that's all.'

It is still a belief with some creative people that all they have to do is have a great idea. It is then up to other people to work out why it is great, and to persuade the client of this greatness. That would be lovely if it were realistic but it isn't. The creative man's responsibility is only half discharged when he's got an idea; he then has to spend at least as much time working out why it's good, why it's relevant – and preferably writing it all down. Certainly, he needs to tell his account man everything he knows about how he arrived at it, and why. The one thing that *isn't* irresponsible, whatever anyone may say, is to write your final strategy after you've done the advertising. Almost every modern writer on the workings of the mind and the process of creation recognises that any new idea is dependent, at some stage, on some sort of accident, on an intuitive leap, which can be rationalised and acknowledged as right only after the event. Edward de Bono says: 'It's sometimes necessary to get to the top of the mountain in order to discover the shortest way up.' I think the same is true for advertising; you may know how to do it only after you've done it. You must try not to cheat, of course – but there's no need to pretend that you wrote your strategy first if you didn't. It's becoming more and more respectable to admit to the truth.

But whether this is worked out before or after the event, it must remain the creative man's inescapable responsibility to know why as well as *what*; and to explain it, preferably in writing.

There are, I believe, only two important reasons for good work failing to be published.

The chief reason is that not nearly enough good work is done in the first place.

The next most important reason is that creative people don't spend nearly enough time helping others understand and imagine what they propose, and why they propose it.

There is, I believe, a final responsibility for the creative man; and that is, paradoxically, somehow to retain a degree of irresponsibility. He is, or should be, the leavening in the account group loaf. He should question accepted premises and turn the obvious upside-down. Most good creative work is done in an atmosphere of enjoyment and excitement. There are times when such an atmosphere ain't that easy to achieve; but it is the creative man's responsibility, I think, to try.

How do I know if I agree
with what we think?

Marketing, November 1997

The client studies another incomprehensible script, the success of which hinges on a blind commitment to half a million pounds' worth of post-production ingenuity. The account executive tells the client for the third time that this is a mould-breaking idea.

'Tell me honestly, Simon,' says the client. 'What do you think?'

'We think it's an absolutely mould-breaking idea,' says the account executive.

'I mean *you*,' says the client. 'I mean *you Simon personally*. What do *you* think?'

Simon chuckles unconvincingly. 'I'm afraid I'm not allowed to tell you what *I* think. I'm only allowed to tell you what *we* think. And we think it's really ballsy, mould-breaking stuff.'

Sam Haskins has been taking excellent photographs for 40-something years. In a recent interview, he was asked his views on the old photography-as-art conundrum. He said, 'Stuff generated by advertising agencies usually dates within a year because most things conceived by a committee have in-built obsolescence.'

The quality that most agencies strive for in their work is distinctiveness. Yes, of course: it has to be relevant, it has to be 'on message' – but distinctiveness is what clients say they want and distinctiveness is what agencies honestly strive to provide. How curious, then, is this tendency to group-think; this addiction to the first-person plural; this clinging to the life-raft of the corporate we.

How would you feel about a director or a photographer or a Queen's Counsel or a neuro-surgeon who never told you what they, personally, thought? We go to them for singular, first-person views and talents; not to act as obedient representatives of some invisible cabinet. So why not to advertising agencies?

Because, I fear, today's account executive is only rarely respected as an advertising expert. And the decline in the standing of the agency account executive and the decline in the standing of the agency itself are closely related. How can a client trust his principal adviser when his adviser doesn't know what he thinks? Or does know what he thinks, but isn't allowed to say what he thinks? Or has to go back and consult his agency in order to find out what he is authorised to think?

How many times must a client suspect that, in his heart of hearts, Simon thinks this really ballsy, mould-breaking stuff is a steaming mound of self-indulgence?

Haskins is of course right: exceptional work is far more likely to emerge from individuals than from committees. But advertising is not art; ideas, once born, must always be constructively challenged. 'Trust me, I'm an art director' is an inadequate basis for the disposition of several million pounds of someone else's money.

The trouble with the corporate we is not that it exists, but that it's all too often used in the mindless defence of the mediocre, rather than in the convinced and exultant promotion of an outstanding idea, rigorously examined.

Archimedes and the efficacy of prayer
Some thoughts on how we think of
things and put them to the test

Advertising agencies are paid by clients to think of things. They have to think of new products, advertising ideas, headlines for advertisements, new ways to reach people. On the grounds that if you have some idea of how people do think of things you have a better chance of encouraging them to do it either more frequently or more rapidly or both, I began to give a lot of thought to the process of invention – and was much helped, influenced, reassured and entertained by the work of Sir Peter Medawar. A friend had lent me *The Art of the Soluble* which I greatly enjoyed, and I was then prompted by a piece by Bernard Levin to read *Induction and Intuition in Scientific Thought*. I also did my best to read Arthur Koestler's *The Act of Creation*. It's full of good things (far better, I think, than Medawar's uncharacteristically vicious review might suggest), although immensely dense and repetitive. Medawar also led me to Karl Popper, to whom Bryan Magee (in his Fontana Modern Masters' *Popper*) proved an invaluable guide. Throughout this process of exploration, I remained acutely conscious of the pretension factor: of seeming to suggest that a new advertising campaign for canned pineapples was of the same order of importance as the discovery of the first non-toxic anti-bacterial agent. It just seemed to me then, and still does, quite interesting that the processes of thought that led to both seem uncannily close, if not identical. The following piece started life in 1985 as an after-dinner speech to a Unilever conference and later became an address to the Account Planning Group in London, in November of the same year.

Let me start with Archimedes because everyone knows about him. Not only did he invent a particular kind of drill, but he also leapt out of his bath shouting 'Eureka!' Not many people know much more than that about Archimedes – but there is quite a lot more to know which, as they say in the States, I'd now like to share with you.

Archimedes worked for a man called Hiero who was the then Tyrant of Syracuse. Hiero was the protector and

Archimedes was, to translate only a little freely, his creative consultant.

One day, a Wednesday I believe, Hiero received a gift from a neighbouring tyrant whom Hiero didn't altogether trust. The gift was a most beautiful and intricate crown – allegedly made of gold. But was it really gold – pure gold – or was it an alloy? Hiero, like all experienced clients, had his doubts.

'Tell me,' Hiero said to Archimedes, 'you're my consultant – and I don't have to remind you that there are plenty more where you came from. Tell me – is this crown pure gold, or is it, as I suspect, adulterated with silver? You've got till Monday.'

That was the brief: and a good deal better than most, I have to say. But what does Archimedes do next? It's clear that science is needed: and logic and deduction.

As I'm sure you will have appreciated, in order to meet his brief, Archimedes needed to establish two facts: the *weight* of the crown and its *volume.*

Establishing the weight presented no problem – he already knew the specific weight of pure gold, but what about its volume? How can you accurately measure the volume of a solid object as complicated as a filigreed crown?

As a matter of fact, it's a doddle: you simply melt it down into a cube and measure that.

'Excuse me, Hiero. Good news I'm happy to say. It is gold. Or, to put it another way, it *was* gold. Had to boil it up, I'm afraid. Still – I cracked it.'

That would have been a vertical, logical, scientific solution, but Archimedes was quick to spot the disadvantages.

He spent several sleepless nights. The problem never went away. At some level of consciousness, it was lurking there in his mind. It preoccupied him, in the proper sense of that word.

The days passed. Monday was getting closer. His contract with Hiero was due to be re-negotiated. He read speculation in the trade press that Hiero was inviting other creative consultants to come in and give him credentials presentations. And then he got into his bath.

Now, history is not clear on this point, but there's nothing in contemporary literature to suggest that this was the *first* bath that Archimedes had ever taken. The chances are that he'd had several; possibly one a day; perhaps as many as thousands. So he must have noticed more than once that when he got in, the water level went up; and that when he got out, the water level went down.

Indeed, he must not only have noticed this phenomenon, he must have been affected by it. He must have said to his valet or his handmaiden: 'Don't fill my bath to the top, you fool, because if you do, it will overflow on to the floor when I get in and there'll be hell to pay from herself underneath.'

But this time, he not only noticed, he *connected*. The further he lowered himself into the bath, the higher the water level and vice-versa. That is why – and when – he shouted 'Eureka!'

Even that new information, of course, leaves out quite a lot. Because at some point – at the risk of being laborious about this – his mind must have gone through the following process:

'My body is a complicated solid. When I put it into water, the level goes up. The more of it I put in, the higher the level. There must therefore be a connection between my volume and the water displaced. If I could measure the water levels both before and after my total immersion, I would have measured the precise equivalent of my own volume. But I can't because my bath is not geometrical in shape: but it could be if it was square and straight-sided. So if I take a geometrically-shaped vessel, half fill it with water, mark the level, drop in that bloody crown, mark the new level and then measure the cubic difference – I'll know the precise volume of the crown. I think …'

I can't tell you whether that process of thought took Archimedes a few minutes or a few hours or a few seconds – but he must have gone through it. And I can't tell you whether he dropped the crown into a square-sided container or a cylindrical container – though it's interesting to reflect that a cylinder wouldn't have been much use to him unless Pythagoras had already had his own Eureka moment with πR^2.

So what do we learn from the full, true story of Archimedes?

I would suggest the following.

— First, that 'pure' observation, even if exists, is a total waste of time; it is without use. (There is the story of the well-educated person of the last century who recorded everything he observed, every day, during the full course of his adult life. And on his death he left these observations to the British Museum where, as far as I know, they still reside. Nobody has yet found them to be at all useful for anything because they had no shape, were based on no hypothesis, contained no insights and made no connections.)

— Observation is of value only when the observer is obsessed by a problem, and when that obsession is sustained, at whatever level of consciousness, by an internal or external *something*: fear, vanity, competition, money, curiosity, desperation or a deadline.

— Everything observed under these circumstances is *potentially relevant*. The observation is not pure: connections are being sought between the obsession and the phenomenon. Some of the techniques employed in synectics, in brainstorming, and the random input/stimulus game recommended by Edward de Bono are no more nor less than deliberate attempts to replicate this instinctive process. Ask a writer to write a story and he may not know how to begin. Ask the same writer to write a story about (at random) an international terrorist and a tube of Smarties and he'll soon get started. It may not be a very *good* story, but ideas don't have to be good to qualify as ideas.

— Once that connection – or possible connection – has been forged, it generates not discovery, and certainly not justification, but *hypothesis*. If this is so, then does it follow that…?

— That hypothesis then needs to be proved – in the proper sense of probed or put to the test. The expression 'the exception that proves the rule' isn't as fatuous as it sounds because it doesn't mean what most people think it means at all: it means the exception that tests the rule, that challenges the rule. Is it a rule at all? And the proof of the pudding is the test of the pudding – not its alcoholic strength.

— And *then* you say: could I have arrived at this hypothetical conclusion sequentially, logically, deductively? If the answer is yes, then that hypothesis can be entertained at a higher level of certainty.

So what's my authority for all this assertion (and there's lots more to come)?

I've always been interested in what's called 'the creative process' but have found it quite difficult to track down any decent books about it. Arthur Koestler's *The Act of Creation* (all 700 pages of it) is hard going but worth it; and I'm indebted to him for the true story of Archimedes. But, such is our culture gap, for many years I looked for books only under the heading of 'Arts'. My reasoning was simple: I'd never been able to do long division; therefore all Science was incomprehensible; therefore I was Arts; therefore Arts and Science had nothing in common. I don't know if this is a savage indictment of our educational system or a savage indictment of me.

So it was mainly by chance that I stumbled on the work of P.B. Medawar or Professor Peter Medawar, now Sir Peter Medawar. Other than by chance, how would I have found myself reading a book by a distinguished immunologist, a joint Nobel prizewinner, with the irresistible title of *Induction and*

Intuition in Scientific Thought? And not only reading it, but going through it as if it were *The Day of the Jackal*?

It was in truth only part chance – like Archimedes' bath. That book, and another by Medawar called *The Art of the Soluble,* had commanded my attention because I'd been trying to work out for myself how we thought of things and put them to the test. The apparently irrelevant connected.

From Medawar I learned that, for 150 years, the only respectable and respected scientists were those who arrived at some new conclusion or truth as the result of a step-by-step, logical sequence of thought, in which every step was dependent on the demonstrable validity of its predecessor. This is what I had always thought – and it scared me because I couldn't do long division and I couldn't think like that, so I knew I wasn't scientific.

Then Medawar told me that, in real life, it wasn't like that at all. That was simply how scientific papers were written.

This is Medawar: 'Scientific papers in the form in which they are communicated to learned journals are notorious for misrepresenting the processes of thought that led to whatever discoveries they describe.' That was magic. That was marketing case histories. That was truth. I wanted more.

But before that, and only partly because it's been some time since I mentioned him, back to Archimedes.

Think how his introduction to a paper in a learned journal might have read: 'The task of measuring the volume of complicated solids has perplexed scientists for centuries.

'We approached the problem logically, objectively and deductively. We reasoned that a solid object was no more nor less than the temporary formation of a liquid, as ice is to water. Theoretically, therefore, all that was required was a methodology allowing a solid to become a notional liquid for the purposes of measurement. Since volume by definition implies space occupied, it followed that space occupied *within a liquid* allowed for the measurement of the volume of liquid both before and after the total immersion of the object in question. The difference between the two, which for the purposes of this paper we shall denominate "displacement", therefore equalled the volume of the solid immersed. The only requirement thereafter was the choice of a vessel of the requisite size and of a shape that was readily susceptible to conventional linear measurement.'

Archimedes should be ashamed of himself.

Doesn't that square precisely with Medawar's assertion that 'scientific papers in the form in which they are communicated to learned journals are notorious for misrepresenting the processes of thought that led to whatever discoveries they describe?' Isn't that account planners after the event? Isn't that *Admap*? Isn't that the IPA Advertising Effectiveness Awards? Isn't that all of us?

But, of course, the discovery is valid; only the process has been falsified. So does it matter? I would argue: yes, it does, very much.

Because this kind of all-too-familiar rubbish, perpetrated I have to concede not only by scientists and account planners, leads to a fusion and a blurring of two quite distinct stages in the development of an idea. And the two stages are: *discovery* (or believed discovery); and *justification.*

It is not true that as someone once said, 'that which leads us to form an opinion is also that which justifies our holding that opinion.'

To believe in the thought processes described by the scientific papers or the marketing case histories is to be encouraged to approach the next new problem in a manner that makes it least likely to be solved. And that's why it matters.

From all of Medawar, and from his mentor and inspiration, Sir Karl Popper, the concept of *hypothesis* comes out proud and strong. Poor old hypothesis – despised for a century and usually preceded by the qualification 'mere' as in: 'That, my dear Archimedes, is mere hypothesis.' I hope it is now restored to its true and rightful position.

Another great and famous scientist – whose name I've forgotten – said this: 'The generative act is the formulation by a hypothesis. We must entertain some hypothesis or else forgo all further knowledge. Hypothetical reasoning is the only kind of argument which starts a new idea.' I have to say that in real life, however big or trivial the problem, I've never known an exception to that statement.

First, then, discovery: the generation of hypotheses. The generators of hypotheses are intuition, induction, desperation, muddle, luck, random associations, indiscipline and preoccupation. But what happens then?

The answer is always, the opposite: the rigorous application of deductive discipline.

I'm also indebted to Sir Peter Medawar for the story of one of Britain's earliest speculative scientists, Sir Francis Galton.

At some point in the 1860s, and I'm afraid I can't tell you why, Sir Francis became obsessively curious about *prayer*. He observed that a great many people prayed, and that most of them prayed *for* something. But did prayer, he wondered, really work? So in a pure, detached, speculative state of mind he set out to test its demonstrable efficacy.

You should remember that he had available to him no computer, no research budget and no Archimedes. The only data available to him were published data.

His first step was to note that millions of people every day prayed for the health and longevity of members of the Royal Family. Did those prayers, he wondered, have any measurable effect?

So he went back a hundred years or more and totted up the mean terminal age of all those members of the Royal Family who had expired during that period. But that in itself, of course, was of no value: he needed comparison. Being a scrupulous person, he knew it would be questionable to compare the mean terminal age of members of the Royal Family with that of the population as a whole, since many were poor, malnourished and had little access to medical care.

So he went as a source to the *General Biographical Dictionary* (32 volumes) and the *Annual Register* and added up the ages at death of eminent men, and the gentry, and officers of the Royal Navy and members of the prosperous professions. He found that the average age at death of members of the Royal Family, when compared with that of prosperous persons of somewhat humbler birth, was slightly lower. (You'll be pleased to know that in each group his sample size was of an order to make them statistically significant.)

But then Sir Francis said to himself: 'Have I missed something out? I don't know if it exists or not and I don't know how to quantify it: but it could well be that an essential factor in effective prayer is the presence of something called sincerity. And maybe when people pray for the health and longevity of the Royal Family, it's more rote than religion. But surely,' he thought further, 'that elusive quality called sincerity must be present when people pray for the health of their unborn children.' So he went back to the *Times*, a paper read by the professional classes generally, and he also went to a paper called the *Record*, which was the trade paper of the clergy. He found that the proportion of stillbirths recorded in each was precisely the same: there was no evidence whatsoever that the prayers of the devout were any more effective than those of the pagan.

His third and last hypothesis strikes me as the most brilliant of all. 'What about *annuities*?' he said to himself. 'The price of annuities is based most carefully by actuaries on the likely longevity of the purchaser. The longer the likely life, the higher the price. What's more,' he said to himself, 'the Quakers are an interesting lot. Not only are they profoundly devout, but they have also got something of a corner in the insurance business.'

So Sir Francis went to the Quakers and said, 'Tell me: how much more do you charge for an annuity to a fellow Quaker?'

And the Quakers said, 'We're not entirely sure we understand the question.'

In 1872, Sir Francis Galton published his findings under the title *Statistical Inquiries into the Efficacy of Prayer* – and all hell broke loose.

Nobody at the time could believe that Galton's inquiry was prompted purely by scientific curiosity. Nobody admired his imagination, his clarity of critical thought or his wonderful methodology. I think we should.

One of the toughest truths to come to terms with in the generation of ideas and the testing of them is the difference between validation and invalidation. All human instinct says, when you've got an idea, try to *validate* it.

But it was Popper again, I think, who was the first to point out the absence of symmetry between validation and invalidation; and he used this example. Your assumption may be, your hypothesis may be, that all swans are white. That's the idea. And you may spend the rest of your life observing white swans – twenty, six hundred, five thousand. But at no point can you say that your assumption has been validated. All you can do, with each white swan observed, is to entertain your hypothesis with a slightly higher level of confidence. But should you observe just one black swan, your hypothesis is dead. Unlike validation, invalidation is finite, clean and immediate.

Invalidation is therefore of huge value: the debate is over, your hypothesis was wrong and you need to modify or start again. Invalidation stops you wasting your time.

But at the time, of course, it isn't always terrifically welcome. You go back to your group or your client and you say: 'Great news! Just been to the research debrief and we've invalidated the idea completely!'

What all this theory is called, as I'm sure you know, is the hypothetico-deductive method of scientific thought. In brief, to recapitulate, what it says is this:

— We must make a clear distinction between *discovery* (or believed discovery) and *proof* – in its proper sense. The elementary act is having an idea. Techniques and pressures and preoccupation can help – but the process of having an idea is neither logical nor illogical: it is *alogical*, it is *outside* logic and cannot be made the subject of logical rules. For all that, the process is respectable, scientific, necessary and part of a demonstrable scientific methodology.

— Having been generated, hypotheses must be criticised and tested. If we can invalidate in the light of observable phenomena (black swans) we feed back, modify or start again; but at the very least with a greater body of knowledge. The failure to invalidate does not imply validation: it just allows us to entertain that hypothesis with an ever-growing level of conviction.

— And of course, it may not be 'right' for ever – just the best available for a long time. It was a long time between Newton and Einstein – and in all probability, Einstein's got it coming to him yet.

As a way of thinking about things and putting them to the test, the hypothetico-deductive system itself may not be right for ever, but it does, as a model, have many advantages. By making that clear distinction between discovery and justification, it gets away from that sterile argument about logic and intuition, between creative brilliance and marketing as a science.

We need to be intuitive, instinctive, scared and lucky. *And* we need to be rigorous, disciplined, logical and deductive. Both kinds of mind and thought are required: the trick is to recognise which kind we need – and, just as importantly, when we need it.

Most of all this came from Medawar. If you'd like to check my sources, I recommend a book containing a large part of his writing (including *Induction and Intuition in Scientific Thought*). It's called *Pluto's Republic*. As he reveals in the introduction, he once went to a party in the country and was introduced to a fellow guest who said, 'Ah, Professor Medawar. You're something of a philosopher I understand. Don't you just adore Pluto's *Republic*?' And because he's a man of wit as well as thought, he chose that as an entirely appropriate title for his collected writing.

The only trouble is, of course, that the irony of it escapes almost everybody.

What are advertising agencies for?
The lesson of the frozen lasagne

The following is an presentation from the Institute of Practitioners in Advertising conference at Cabot Hall, Canary Wharf in October 1992. In retrospect, the roaring 80s can be seen as a time of over-confidence and under-investment in British advertising agencies. When the fall came, it was painful. Advertising expenditures were cut. Many people lost their jobs (between 1988 and 1992, IPA agencies cut staff by 15 per cent). And something less measurable but no less worrying seemed to have happened to the agency/client relationship. Agencies felt they had become less central, less trusted and less valued. The 1992 IPA conference set out to examine and confront this issue. Six years later, the topic is still a live one.

This is the second most daunting thing I've been asked to do by the IPA this year – so I thought I'd spend most of my time talking about the *most* daunting thing I was asked to do by the IPA this year. This has two advantages: one, thrift; and two, more surprisingly, relevance.

The most daunting thing was being asked to be one of the judges of the 1992 IPA Advertising Effectiveness Awards. Now, at some considerable risk to my own reputation – particularly throughout the fairly dreadful 1980s – I've always been strongly and openly in favour of these awards. And, as I hardly need remind you, this *was* a highly risky attitude to adopt because that was the time when to be openly in favour of advertising effectiveness was to declare yourself tyrannically opposed to something called creativity.

To those of you over 50 or under 25, this may seem a statement of extreme improbability – but the rest of you will know that it's true.

Advertising agencies publicly wondered out loud if they should position themselves as 'marketing' agencies – meaning, they should concern themselves with their clients' businesses;

or as 'creative' agencies – meaning they should concern themselves only with the number of creative awards they could acquire. The concept of creativeness and the concept of effectiveness became alternatives – or worse. As Bernard Barnett wrote in *Campaign* last November: 'I am fed up with the increasingly common treatment of "creativity" and "effectiveness" as antonyms.'

But while creativity and effectiveness are certainly not antonyms, neither of course are they synonyms.

A very long time ago, four of us from different advertising agencies, sponsored by Unilever, made a cheap little black-and-white film called *Risk & Responsibility*. It was compered by Ronnie Kirkwood – and practically the first thing he did was to show the camera the front page of a daily newspaper and say (and I paraphrase):

'Whichever agency buys this space, the cost to the client is going to be about the same. However, the *value* to that client of buying that space will vary enormously according to which words and which pictures he decides to fill it with.'

The word 'creativity' can mean a lot of things to a lot of people: but at least in its very limited advertising sense, it can surely mean only one quite specific thing. It means the inventiveness and the skill with which expensive time or space, which if left empty would be worthless, can be coaxed into returning more that their cost to the advertiser. The more creative the advertisement, the greater the return.

Effectiveness is about *why* you advertise: you want to have an effect. Creativity is about *how* you advertise. Neither antonyms nor synonyms: the first is an end, and the second a means to that end.

Such art as there is in advertising is an *applied* art: it is there to do something, to achieve something. It may, incidentally, be admired for itself; and that may in itself have a secondary value to the advertiser. But it must never, never be the primary aim. It is never an end in itself.

Which is why the task of helping to judge this year's IPA Advertising Effectiveness Awards, though certainly daunting, has, to my considerable astonishment, been as exciting for me as being on a treasure hunt.

And it seemed to me, in trying to clarify what value today's agencies can bring to clients' businesses, it would be a great deal better to talk about the certainties of some of these specific, rock-solid recent achievements than to embark on any number of chunter-chunter generalities.

In each of the 30 or more short-listed submissions, all closely argued and running to several thousand words each, a clear and common pattern emerges.

First: an objective is defined. And that's the first shocking reminder, because we keep on forgetting just how varied advertising objectives can be. They may be as simple as wanting more people to buy more things more often – but only very seldom. From the short-list alone, here are a few: to present a new car so that it appeals to a group of people known to be indifferent to the car's manufacturer; to protect profit margins; to bring a brand with an old-fashioned reputation up-to-date; to help insurance brokers, the intermediaries, find ready acceptance when proposing a particular policy; to increase the number of visitors to Whipsnade; to raise money for Save the Children; to slow the decline of the door-to-door milkman; to enter a market; to prevent a competitor from entering a market; to attract fewer, higher-spending customers; to persuade more parents to have their children inoculated; to prevent the Canadian Government from culling seals.

It's very clear from these papers that the defining of a realistic advertising objective is already part of the creative process, and that an agency begins to earn its money as soon as it brings its imagination to bear – even at this stage.

And then, after the objective, comes the idea – quite often, the Big Idea. In every single one of the papers I've read, the Big Idea is simply stated, or shown or reproduced.

Fascinatingly, nobody ever attempts to explain how those ideas came about in the first place. They are all miraculous virgin births – which only after delivery can be seen to make sense.

And I make that point not to mock. Any paper that pretended to explain the logical, linear process of thought that led to an original advertising idea would almost certainly be misleading if not actually a lie. But it's still a bit of a pity, it seems to me, that the advertising agency's greatest single justification for existence – the generation of ideas that contribute so powerfully to the advertisers' own aims – should have to be so perfunctorily covered. All we know is that, by some mysterious process, somebody somewhere thought of the dancing milk bottles and Stella's 'reassuringly expensive' and the Häagen Dazs couple who can think of nothing but ice cream, and Renault's Nicole and Papa, and skip-a-lunch for Save the Children, and the Andrex puppy, and the wonderful misfortunes of Scottish Amicable. In every one of those short-listed entries, there's an idea that more than paid for itself. And that, of course, is not just the view of the agency itself: it's a view held with equal conviction by the people who paid for it all – the clients – without whose willing agreement these entries couldn't have been submitted.

And in some of these true stories, there are examples of ideas which have gone on for years and years: protecting margins, contributing to profit, confirming loyalty, resisting competitive challenges and helping to underwrite brand extensions. Someone, for example, should give a special award to the late and remarkable Leo Burnett for having invented, as long ago as 1936, the Jolly Green Giant: an improbable character who must by now have contributed many billions of dollars to the Minnesota Valley Canning Company.

But for me, the really telling lesson that comes through virtually every one of these remarkable stories is yet another reminder: a reminder about the nature of *brands* and the contribution that grown-up advertising can make to them.

Because the best of the ideas I've talked about are not just *advertising* ideas: they're *brand* ideas.

They provide the most potent of clues from which consumers – real people – can construct in their heads and their hearts a simple and coherent assessment of objects as inanimate as a can of sweetcorn or as intangible as an insurance company.

The word 'brand' has become so fashionable that we've stopped thinking what it means; we now use it almost interchangeably with the word 'product'. And the inevitable consequence of this bit of mental laziness can be seen in a great deal of advertising which seems not even to have tried to epitomise clearly defined brand values but is content to be simply product advertising. So the style of these advertisements is not the style of the brand: it is the style of the film director or the art director or the last-but-one award winner. And so opportunities are missed and money is wasted. If this is what the first Lord Leverhulme was talking about, he was right.

In good brand advertising, every single executional decision is taken consciously and for a good reason. Certainty about the unique nature of a brand (and if it isn't unique, it isn't a brand) means that the typeface, the voice-over, the casting, the colours, the prose style, the size and length of the ad itself – every single element, however apparently insignificant – combines with the others to contribute to and strengthen that particular brand's competitive personality. Because it's that competitive personality that makes it more desirable, that makes it good value, that inspires affection as well as respect, and that allows it to make a nonsense of traditional life cycle theories.

It must, of course, be the advertiser's responsibility to see that a competitive brand personality is first developed and then meticulously tended and nourished: it's one of the most precious assets a business can have – and you can't (or you shouldn't) sub-contract responsibility for it. But of all an advertiser's many suppliers, his advertising agency should be the one best-positioned and best-equipped to help him invent that personality – and then, through the kind of idea we've been talking about, to give it life and potency and expression.

And it seems to me almost self-evident that, the greater the changes we see happening all around us, in both kind and quantity, the more important that central agency contribution will become.

More choice means more consumer confusion – which means a greater need for brand distinction. More media means more messages – which means a greater need for brand clarity. More international competition means higher entry costs for new products – which means a greater need for brand strength.

Increasing costs and competition mean there will be far fewer free-standing brands launched in future – those orphan brands who seem to have no parents. New brands, to pay back, will need a heritage, an authority, to be seen to come from a decent family. So, in many ways, the battle for consumer respect and affection will become a battle between companies: and every marketing company will need to pay as much attention to its own competitive *corporate* reputation as it has traditionally paid to the personalities of its competing brands.

At the same time, service companies – particularly, perhaps, in financial services – will be looking to achieve the same objective: an overall, distinctive and competitive personality that greatly aids the marketing of near-parity products.

All this, to me, suggests the need for an even closer working relationship between advertiser and agency: a relationship that should start further back in time and further back upstream, when the tentative formulation of a company's long-term strategy is first debated; because that's when the development of its own positioning, the hunt for its own desired personality, can most benefit from the introduction of communications – from words and sounds and pictures and ideas.

I sense, however, that this is not happening: that, if anything, the advertiser/agency relationship has become less close and less central. If so, it is equally bad news for both parties: never have marketing companies been more in need of inspired communications.

If I am right, and the value of advertising and advertising agencies has become less rather than more apparent to advertisers, there's one possible explanation that occurs to me – and I'll call it the lesson of the frozen lasagne.

One of the submissions to this year's IPA Advertising Effectiveness Awards tells the story of the frozen lasagne that increased its sales by 180 per cent, going from fourth brand to first in the same period. Convincingly, much of the credit for this remarkable achievement is attributed to one television commercial – and the interesting thing about that commercial is this: against a great deal of conventional wisdom, it didn't put the case for this *particular* frozen lasagne: it just showed very engagingly how frozen lasagne *as such* met the needs of today's fragmented families. Until that point, all the competing lasagnes had been so totally preoccupied with pointing up their small differences and their own particular peripheral advantages that consumers – real people – remained reasonably unenthusiastic about the sector itself. No one had told them of the glories and satisfactions of the market as a whole.

I do hope that you out there this morning won't mind too much being compared to frozen lasagnes – because I think it's likely that we have much to learn from them.

We've all been so busy promoting our own agencies, our differences, our own particular philosophies and facilities, that the market – the advertisers – have remained reasonably unenthusiastic about the sector in general. No one has reminded them of the values and glories of the market as a whole.

If this full day in Canary Wharf is the beginning of an attempt to remedy that omission – and if it's half as successful as the frozen lasagnes were – we shall all have much to smile about in a couple of years' time.

Ten tried and trusted ways of getting the least from your advertising agency

Agencies find their clients invaluable as scapegoats for undistinguished advertising. Clients are accused of over-reliance on research, of cowardice, of demanding original ideas that have already been proved effective in the marketplace. Agencies that lack confidence blame their clients far too much: it is, after all, the agency's job not only to invent the right campaign in the first place but also to persuade its client to run it. But, as all clients should agree, the primary responsibility for a healthy and productive agency relationship must lie with the principal, the client himself. Clients (and individuals within client companies) differ widely in their appreciation of this fact and in their ability to do anything about it. The following piece started life as a presentation to a Johnson Wax marketing seminar on Rhodes in June 1978. Thirteen years later, when the speech was being prepared for the first edition of this book, it was observed that there were actually eleven tried and trusted ways, not ten. I had put in two number tens and nobody had noticed. In the interests of historical accuracy, we have kept it that way.

You have asked me to speak on the subject of client/agency relationships. I was initially tempted to talk at very great length about mother-love and mutual trust and partnerships and shared goals – but before I had time to get down to the clichés, I read a piece in *Campaign* by Tom Rayfield who is one of our creative supervisors at J. Walter Thompson, London. His article was called 'How to make the least of your advertising agency' which struck me as an altogether more promising approach. So what I've done, with his permission, is adapt his title. The content which follows is mine; so I wouldn't want you to take it out on Tom afterwards.

I shall take you through, one by one, my ten tried and trusted ways of getting the least from your advertising agency – every one of which I've personally experienced and can therefore warmly recommend. I have to admit that few clients, however dedicated, have mastered all ten – though the simultaneous use of five or six is not unusual. But if you listen carefully, and take notes, you could be the first client in the world to bring your agency to an hysterical, bankrupt standstill.

Method No 1: Keep them feeling insecure.

Advertising agencies, even big ones, are very small businesses. If they're any good, they'll have on their payroll an unusually large number of sensitive, talented, fallible, competitive and insecure people.

If there are 50 people working on your account, perhaps three will be motivated by the amount of money you spend with them and the amount of profit they make. (That would be the managing director, the financial director and, only to a limited extent, the person in charge of your account.)

The other 47 will be motivated by an interest in producing good advertising which helps you to be more successful, and by the sheer, fascinating difficulty of doing the job.

By not trusting your agency you can – instantly – *demotivate* all those 47 people whose help (presumably) you need.

An elementary but nonetheless effective strategem is to let it be known that you are visiting other agencies. Not seriously, of course: you're just doing your job by keeping in touch with the marketplace. Ideally, the news of your visits should first reach your agency through the pages of the trade press.

This course of action will have the immediate effect of making your agency devote all its efforts to pleasing you, rather than trying to produce the right answers to your marketing and advertising problems.

All agencies are insecure – and if they aren't, they ought to be. The loss of an account is a serious matter and the agency, quite properly, will usually accept more than 70 per cent of the blame. Any signs of complacency in your agency can quickly be corrected by a short, sharp telephone call and a follow-up letter. But that's sensible. Far more enjoyable to increase their sense of insecurity to the level of mindless dither.

Method No 2: Keep them in the dark.

Tell your agency that you have a fully-staffed, highly professional marketing department and that all you need from them is some advertisements. This technique means that you can legitimately keep from your agency such irrelevant information as sales figures, research data, competitive activity and any other knowledge you may have about the nature of your market.

However big or small your agency, this kind of relationship can be guaranteed to encourage irrelevant advertising.

It will deny you access to anyone in the agency who might just be able to help you with your marketing planning, and will encourage the agency to assess its own work on some vacuous scale of creativity. Thus at one stroke you screw up the relationship and fail to get the best value for the fees or commissions you pay. Very quickly you will begin to wonder if the agency isn't making more money than you are.

Method No 3: Employ at least one incompetent, underworked junior.

These words are carefully chosen. He or she must be incompetent, underworked *and* junior – otherwise this method has been known to fail.

His job (or to be more accurate, his non-job) is to waste your agency's time. He is *always* in the agency – because in the agency he feels important whereas back in his own office he feels little more than an incompetent, underworked junior.

Ideally, he or she should have a slightly ridiculous Christian name, such as Beverley, so that the agency group can say, 'Oh, Christ. Beverley's in again and wants lunch.'

If he's really incompetent, he can not only waste the agency's time but mislead them. He will gossip continually – about his superiors, their personal habits, their rivalries, what they really think of the agency; and what they thought of the other agencies they've been seeing secretly.

Naturally, any agency with courage, principles and a sound relationship with a more senior client will soon make it clear that Beverley is doing far more harm than good. Equally naturally, the senior client, who has been to management school and knows the importance of being seen to back your own people, will be embarrassed. Also, that week, by sheer chance, the agency will have sent in its first inaccurate invoice for two years.

The courageous, principled agency will therefore find itself immediately on the defensive; the senior client will question Beverley closely about his (or her) views of the agency; Beverley will claim single-handed credit for keeping them on their toes (why else would he need to spend so much time in the agency?); and another close and fruitful partnership will begin to disintegrate. No client with serious ambitions to be bad can afford to be without a Beverley.

Method No 4: Tell different people different things.

You have plenty of scope for doing this if you have a highly structured and graded marketing department, the value of which I shall return to later. It also helps if you are part of a multinational marketing company. This gives you the opportunity to tell the *management* of your agency that the sort of advertising you really want is the sort that Chuck Rebozo will understand back in Akron, Ohio. Meanwhile, your advertising manager is telling the *account executive*, the hell with Chuck Rebozo – what *he* wants is advertising that will shift product in the Philippines.

By the time the agency management and the account executive have exchanged notes, it will be impossible for them to formulate a brief or motivate the creative group.

Another small tip, here. Tell your agency that you are deeply suspicious of any advertising that wins prizes, while simultaneously expressing mild disappointment that the work they do for you never does.

Method No 5: Never put the truth in writing.

A simple technique – and one that seems to come quite naturally to many clients. Write a letter after the first presentation of the creative material congratulating the agency on its fresh and stimulating approach and encouraging them to develop it. *At the same time* instigate a series of internal discussions designed to spread unease and uncertainty among your own people. I strongly recommend phrases such as 'Creativity for its own sake …', 'Certainly all in favour of originality, but …' and 'I can't help wondering what Chuck Rebozo will make of it.'

At all these meetings, make absolutely certain that Beverley is present. You may safely rely on him to do the rest.

When asked at the annual agency/client review your opinion of the account group, reply, in writing, 'Absolutely first-class.' Within a month, ask the managing director of your agency if you could have a word with him sometime on the subject of staffing …

Method No 6: Never admit to a mistake.

This technique has two advantages. First, it keeps your own record clean: important if you are at all ambitious. Even more valuably, it means that your agency will soon adopt the same practice and never admit to a mistake either.

As we all know, the best advertising emerges from a totally open and honest assessment of a brand's strengths and weaknesses, and general agreement on past errors and omissions. With neither side ever admitting to a mistake, this kind of discussion becomes immediately impossible. Mistakes, instead of being swiftly rectified, are perpetuated; and you should be able to look forward quite confidently to inferior and irrelevant work.

Method No 7: Change your main contact with the agency at least once a year.

This can often be achieved without even trying, but check that you aren't inadvertently allowing any really fruitful professional relationships to take root.

Simultaneously, insist that your agency maintains complete stability at their end. This will ensure that only stale minds are brought to bear on your problems.

After three years, and three quite different advertising managers from your side, you should be able to review the work on your brands and demonstrate a sad lack of consistency. And that, of course, is the time to suggest an entirely new agency group – which in turn will guarantee a fourth new campaign in as many years.

Any successful brand must retain some elements of consistency in its advertising. Somebody must, through sheer experience and sensitivity, be the guardian, the custodian, of that brand's essential values. By switching your agency contact frequently, you hand over that responsibility to your agency – which in turn allows you quite justly to accuse them of reluctance to change and a paucity of original thought.

This technique, when mastered, can destroy not only your agency but also your most profitable brands.

Method No 8: Demonstrate a complete absence of concern about agency profitability.

I have said that very few people in an agency are motivated by the amount of money your account makes: and that's true.

However, the really shrewd bad client recognises that the reverse does not necessarily apply.

If everyone in the agency knows that: a) you've asked for four different creative groups to work on your Christmas promotion; b) you plan to spend virtually nothing on that promotion; c) your account has been a financial haemorrhage for five years; and d) you don't care – then you've pulled off a neat trick. You've turned people who only care about standards into people who only care about money.

And while on this subject, asking for four separate creative groups to work on your account is worth bearing in mind even if – despite your best efforts – the account remains profitable. There's a simple law called The Law of Diminishing Responsibility. The more people you ask to think about a problem, the less time and thought and commitment each will feel required to apply. You therefore get four superficial solutions at four times the expense of one excellent solution. You will find Beverley particularly valuable at moments like this, since he will have the time to mislead even more people than usual.

Method No 9: Never say thank you.

As I'm sure you know, good agency people are fuelled and refuelled mainly by gratitude, encouragement and appreciation.

A word of advice: *starve them of it.*

It should always be too early to say thank you – or too late. Your campaign may not work; or it was done so long ago that by now you've changed your agency contact.

One handwritten letter thanking your account executive or creative director could bring you enough enthusiasm and commitment to keep up a flow of good advertising for another year – and what really bad client wants *that*, for God's sake?

Method 10: Never pay for a drink.

This is far more important that it may seem at first glance. It doesn't just confirm your agency's view of your essential mean-spiritedness – though that in itself shouldn't be under-estimated.

More fundamentally, by never buying a drink, you establish beyond doubt your fundamental view of the client/agency relationship. None of this partnership rubbish we hear so much about. The relationship is one of principal and supplier, master and servant.

The function of a supplier, it stands to reason, is to supply: ideas, advertising, specially designed birthday cards for your chairman's wife. And drinks.

A supplier is by definition inferior to a principal, and why should you waste your company's money buying drinks for inferiors?

And if you *did* buy them a drink, they might think you quite liked them or appreciated them or something – and we all know what that could lead to. The same old trap: good work.

And finally:

Second Method 10: Install a highly complex, hierarchical approval system.

Naturally, you can only be certain of what sort of system to adopt if you first understand how good advertising can sometimes slip through by mistake.

As I think we've recognised before at these seminars, good advertising is most likely to be produced by a combination of disciplined and shared thinking about strategy, and the undisciplined, unfettered, uninhibited search for ideas. It may well be – indeed, it often is – the case that only in the search for the solution will the true problem be fully recognised and understood. In other words, in the creative process, an element of muddle, of experiment, of feedback, of modification, of trial and error, and of mutual trust and a shared excitement in discovery are all essential if problem and solution are to be elegantly and successfully resolved.

Your approval system, therefore, must ensure that none of this, under any circumstances, is possible.

I have two suggestions which I hope you find helpful. Neither is original, I'm afraid – but I've never been too proud to steal other people's ideas as long as they're bad ones.

First: insist not only that a communications strategy is written down and agreed – that's reasonable. Go further: make it clear that any deviation from that strategy, particularly in the event of new insights and understanding emerging, is at all times prohibited.

Second: in your hierarchy of approval, have as many different levels as you can reasonably afford and *always start at the bottom.*

Naturally enough, Beverley comes in handy here. Because he or she is only 23 and knows nothing about advertising, he must see all the agency's work first. Vest in him the right to say 'no'. (For most Beverleys this is unnecessary: they appropriate such power anyway.) Do not, of course, allow him to say 'yes'.

After he's sent the work back three times for revision, he should allow it to be seen by his two superiors. It's always more effective if they can see the work at different times, and when one of them is going to be out of the country for the next ten days, so they can't consult. They can then put their conflicting views in writing for the agency to consider.

Then I recommend a committee: as large as possible and preferably chaired by the managing director who has to keep leaving the room to talk to major retailers and trades union leaders. The client's people should be on one side of the table, agency people on the other. (A detail, I agree, but these things are important.)

Even more crucial: no one from the client side should admit to having already seen the work, let alone to supporting it.

The agency presents. There is a pause. The managing director (if he's in the room) says, 'Very interesting. What's your view, Beverley?'

From that moment on, everything should flow smoothly. No one is going to say anything that means anything until they know what the managing director thinks. And the managing director isn't going to know what he thinks until he's heard all the others not saying what they think.

The changes insisted on by Beverley are challenged by the marketing director. Beverley invites the agency to defend these changes.

The managing director calls on the sales director who says he's not really qualified to speak on behalf of the consumer but he doesn't think it would go down very well with his sales force who prefer cartoons.

Eventually the managing director sums up. 'It would seem,' he says, 'that there's not total unanimity about these proposals' – and then goes on to suggest that, while the recommendation is by no means dead, there does seem to be a case for the agency asking a second group to work to the same brief so that the committee would be in a position to consider two or more alternatives.

And at that stage, if there is still no sign of general agreement being reached, perhaps some method of formal pre-testing technique should be considered …?

So those are my ten tried and trusted ways of getting the least from your advertising agency. In all fairness, I think you should be given equal time to make a presentation to me: which you might like to call 'ten tried and trusted ways of infuriating your client'.

[This last challenge was accepted – and very funny and chastening it was, too.]

What are account planners for, Daddy?

Account planning, in both name and function, came into being in a few London advertising agencies in the 1960s. The two individuals most properly credited with its introduction are the late, great Stanley Pollitt of Boase Massimi Pollitt, and Stephen King of J. Walter Thompson, by far the best planner I ever worked with. By 1978, the date of the following piece, there were enough account planners in London agencies to justify the formation of a society – the Account Planning Group. Although never a planner myself (other than by instinct) I was invited to address their inaugural meeting. Doubts and self-doubts continue to surround planning and planners. Some agencies have never adopted it as a discrete discipline. A few have abandoned it. American agencies, in the main, have found no compelling reasons for introducing it. Twenty years on, I don't think there's a lot I would either change or add. There is still, to my knowledge, no commonly agreed and commonly used job definition. I note, but without apology, that I've again used James Webb Young's definition of an Advertising Man. See *What Jim Young said* (page 135).

It was kind of you to invite me to give you my personal view of account planning. I have found it a useful exercise. I have now worked with account planners for ten years less one day and I've never – until this evening – been forced to work out in my own mind exactly what my personal opinion of account planning is. I very much agree with A.J.P. Taylor when he says that the only reason he writes is to discover what he thinks.

I suppose the greatest difficulty I've encountered over these ten years is the problem of explaining, first to the creative department and later to clients and potential clients, exactly what an account planner *does*.

The potential client, being a canny fellow and deeply scarred from previous experiences, demands to see the actual, real-life team who would be working on his account. You introduce them.

'This is the director-in-charge,' you say. They nod. They know.

'This is the creative chappie,' you say. They nod. They know.

'And this,' you say, 'is the account planner.' And nobody nods.

At this point you've got two choices. Keep talking or try to explain. I've tried both and neither works.

Keep talking, and the client will say: 'Excuse me, but that's the *who*?' So you end up having to explain anyway.

'I'm glad you asked,' you lie. 'We consider the account planner to be one of the most valuable members of the account group.'

'In what respect?' says the client.

'That's a very good question,' you stall. 'You see, we believe there has to be one member of the account group who knows very precisely, very sensitively, what's going on in the world, in the marketplace, in the consumer's mind.'

'Ah,' says the client, deeply relieved. 'Research person.'

'Well, up to a point and in a manner of speaking, yes. But as such, actually not.'

'In what way not?'

'Well – we were hoping to find time to show you some case histories,' you say, 'and perhaps when you hear the account planner *talk* you'll get a rather clearer idea …'.

But the client insists. Entirely reasonably, he wants to know what the account planner does, why we've got one, how he or she works with the rest of the account group and why the account executive doesn't do the job himself because surely that's part of his job or is he too stupid?

And I have to tell you that, ten years on, having tried several hundred definitions, job descriptions, anecdotes and analogies, I've still not succeeded in explaining, satisfactorily, what the account planner is *for.* Without, that is, simultaneously conveying serious doubts about the adequacy of the rest of the agency and – worse still – the client's own highly trained and expensive marketing department.

There is more than one possible explanation for this dismal record of failure. The first – which I reject out of hand – is my own incompetence. The second is that there *is* no real role for the account planner: an explanation still favoured by some and occasionally, I have to say, when faced with the question, even by me. The third is that – at least until this evening – account planners have themselves failed to define what they are for and what they do.

Which, when you consider what account planners are *supposed* to do, must rank as one of life's richer ironies.

Yet, 12 years ago, there were no account planners. Today, looking around, there are certainly more than that. Could it be that the account planners' greatest achievement to date is – on the basis of there being no satisfactory explanation for their existence – to have lowered by as much as a hundred the unemployment figures in this country?

I must therefore ask two questions. If account planners hadn't been invented, what would you all be doing for a living?

Second: if you *weren't* all account planners, who, if anyone, would be doing what you may or may not have convinced your employers you do all day?

And if, as account planners, you can't provide satisfactory answers to both those questions, you have – in my personal view – totally failed to justify your own existence.

So it could well be that the first, the inaugural, meeting of the Account Planning Group will – to nobody's great surprise – turn out also to be the last.

However, it would I think be churlish and ungrateful of me not to hold out some small flickering hope for your survival, even if I think that in a different sort of world, a simpler and more sensible world, there would indeed be no good reason for your existence.

If you've read the few good books about advertising – and I hope you have, particularly since you have so little else to do all day – you will know that in the twenties and the thirties and the forties and the fifties, particularly in America, there was really only one kind of person of value in an agency. This same character emerges clearly from the work of Claude Hopkins, Albert Lasker, David Ogilvy, Rosser Reeves, James Webb Young and a handful of others.

He or she was not a media man, not an account man, not a creative man and certainly, it goes without saying, not an account planner. He was, quite simply, an Advertising Man.

In his book, *How To Become An Advertising Man*, James Webb Young has this to say: 'The true Advertising Man, as the term is used in this book, is he who has the knowledge, the skills, experience and insights to advise advertisers how best to use advertising to accomplish their objectives. *And* to execute the advertising to do this.'

Notice that Jim Young is referring to an individual – not a group. He expected the Advertising Man, like himself, to be capable of market analysis, competitive analysis, definition of role – *and* creative execution.

Further, he expected this singular individual to acquire seven different categories of knowledge. I quote: 'Knowledge of Propositions, Knowledge of Markets (by which he meant people, not Nielsen), Knowledge of Messages, Knowledge of Carriers of Messages (which means more to me at least than media), Knowledge of Trade Channels, Knowledge of How Advertising Works and, finally, Knowledge of the Specific Situation'.

And that's quite a lot of knowledge for one individual to acquire and apply – even before the days of television rating points, cluster analysis, day-after-recall, the Kelley Repertory Grid and burst-versus-drip.

But even that wasn't enough for Young. He goes on to say: 'No limits can be placed on the kinds of knowledge that are useful to the Advertising Man. Indeed, it can safely be said that the broader his education, and the better stocked his mental pantry, the better at his job he is likely to be. Every really good person in advertising whom I have known has always had two noticeable characteristics. First, there was no subject under the sun in which he could not easily get interested. Second, he was an extensive browser in all sorts of fields.'

Now, as I look, from my personal view, at much of the advertising that's produced in both the States and Britain at the moment, it seems to me to have been produced in total isolation from, and total ignorance of, the real world outside. The prose style used in print copy owes nothing to any other prose style except that used in other print advertisements.

The makers of advertisements appear increasingly to be obsessed by only one subject: their own and other people's advertisements. Increasingly, there is a preoccupation with *advertisements* at the expense of *advertising*.

If true, why has this happened? In all honesty I don't know. The glib and obvious answer may be the right one. The business has become so complicated, so competitive, so specialised, that Jim Young's ideal Advertising Man can no longer realistically be expected to exist.

The account man is obsessed not with the world outside, but with the complexities and language of the grocery market or the electricity supply industry. He has become a surrogate client. The creative man is obsessed not with real people and their wants and desires, but with creativity as an end in itself. And since nobody can tell him what creativity *is,* he is forced to conclude that it is anything that wins the Grand Prix de L'Arc de Triomphe at the Wexford Film Festival.

So, for whatever reason, or set of reasons, the real world outside has become forgotten.

And since one of the prime functions – if not the only function – of most advertising is to build an understanding and sympathetic bridge between the potential supplier and the real world outside, this is a very serious omission indeed. The implications are very clear and very serious: advertising money is likely to be less well spent and the return on the investment of that advertising money will be much reduced. Advertisers will notice; will value advertising less; will divert their limited resources elsewhere: and all of us, of whatever discipline, will quite deservedly suffer.

If I am right in this analysis, then the reason for your existence, and the justification of your pay cheques, begins to become clear.

The account planner – if he does nothing else – must be obsessed with the real world outside; must have a well-stocked mental pantry. There should be no subject under the sun in which he cannot easily become interested.

Then – and this may be more easily said than done – he must represent and illuminate that world outside to the myopic specialists with whom he works. You must be interpreters: but you must interpret in a vivid, evocative, imaginative, allegorical way. Do not give us computer printouts or documents that are appreciated by you on weight and density alone.

At your most valuable, you can illuminate and inspire; you can simplify the complicated; you can provide insights and intuitive hypotheses; and you can clarify and crystallize. You can make sure that your agency remains an *advertising* agency, and does not degenerate into a contracted supplier of commissionable advertisements.

At your least valuable, you can do the reverse. You can complicate the simple, obfuscate the obvious, invent your own language, your own religion, your own self-congratulatory, inward-looking, impenetrable jargon.

So a word of warning if I may, however patronising and unnecessary, about the formation of this group. As members of this group, talking only to each other, you have no value whatsoever. Your *entire* value resides in continuing to be members of working account groups – uncontaminated by too much knowledge of each other.

As people who should be better able than most to imagine what it's like to be *other* people – don't forget what it's like to be an account man or a creative man. Don't forget the *exposure* of the client meeting, the *tyranny* of the blank sheet of paper.

Feel as vulnerable, as committed, as excited, as frightened as the people who've got to produce the ads. Don't sit back smugly after you've written your brief and leave the office at 5:29. Recognise that – however helpful you've been, however useful the insights you've provided – somebody still has to have what is called an Idea.

Please: never forget that knowing you've got to give birth to an idea – however trivial, however small, however unimportant in the greater scheme of things – is very personal and very scary. Never forget that having given birth to one idea and having had it rejected, there is the double fear of not being able to give birth to another.

Please: behave like any understanding, compassionate husband. Hold the hand of your creative partners – and breathe and grunt in rhythm and sympathy.

Share the fright, and share the personal vulnerability. If you don't, you'll soon lose friends and the opportunity and right to influence people.

And then comes evaluation. It may well lie with you, as interpreter again, to report on how the real world accepted, understood and appreciated that small, frail idea that almost certainly wasn't yours in the first place.

To your writer and art director, this can be the equivalent of reading the first edition reviews of a play it's taken two years to write.

Certainly, if the notices are bad, don't lie. But look at them and interpret them with responsible optimism. If there's a genuine flicker of hope, breathe on it gently: don't bash it into extinction with self-satisfied pleasure.

Above all, don't be seen to *disown* an idea just because it becomes apparent it's a rotten idea. Observe carefully your own use of the possessive pronoun. If you talk about 'our' campaign when the results are good, and 'your' campaign when the results are rotten: then you've opted out.

Finally, never forget that advertising and agencies existed without you for over a hundred years and could well exist without you again. Sooner or later, somebody's got to write the words – so, competent or incompetent, there will always be a job for a writer. But if you don't continue to demonstrate your usefulness, your ability to help other people be better at what they do – then, quite simply and quite quickly, you will find yourself unused, unconsulted, unrespected and unhired.

That, in my personal view, is *your* particular discipline's discipline – your vulnerability. You need to be wanted: and that, even more than for most of us, depends on performance.

I believe that you will, and even more fervently, I *hope* that you will. Which is why, almost for the first time in my life, I can say without hypocrisy that I was touched and pleased to be invited to speak at your meeting today.

Account planning and account planners have helped me, educated me, guided me a very great deal. They've continued to remind me that advertising is about effectiveness and results: and that's where our objectives should be, and where our satisfactions should come from.

So may I thank you for having asked me today; may I thank the account planner who provided the imaginative, intuitive, evocative brief on which this speech was based; and may I ask you to let me know, with some urgency, just as soon as you've agreed a comprehensible definition of what an account planner actually *does*?

The case of the missing policeman

After-dinner speech to The Solus Club (an advertising club) at the Hyde Park Hotel in London on 16 November 1989. Edited. Not to be trusted on facts and dates.

I thought what I would do this evening, if that's all right with you, is deliver myself of a bit of a history lesson.

As a matter of fact, even if it's not all right with you, that's what I'm going to do. I thought I would have a look at how the advertising trade has changed – and how attitudes to the advertising trade have changed – over the last 35 years.

I pick 35 years because it is 35 years and one month since I first got paid for being in the advertising trade, and it's also how long that man whose name I forget ran Bulgaria, and only stopped running it six days ago. Isn't that a coincidence?

Thirty-five years and one month is really quite a long period, and I obviously can't do justice to all of it in the time at my disposal this evening. In fact, you'll realise just how sketchy my treatment is going to be when I tell you that I can't really devote much more than a couple of minutes to each year. That is, if we're to have questions. I'm also comforted by the knowledge that most of this splendid audience has been working in advertising far longer than I have. Please feel free therefore to interrupt throughout and correct me on any points of detail, particularly if they are trivial.

In 1954, advertising was still – just – respectable. It was even quite smart. The heroes of short stories in women's magazines quite often worked in advertising agencies, and you couldn't get much smarter than that.

My final interview at J. Walter Thompson was with the chairman. It was the first time I'd ever been inside an office. I'd been summoned from Dunstable Downs where I'd been on a gliding course, and I was feeling very nervous indeed. I can only remember one question the chairman asked me – and for all I know, it was the only question he *did* ask me. 'Tell me, Bullmore,' he said, 'how much money of your own do you have?' You must admit, that's classy. You don't get a chairman these days asking that question – not on the milk round you don't. It's true, as I later discovered, that J. Walter Thompson was a particularly classy agency, but I still think that gives you a bit of the flavour of the 1950s. A youngish BBC producer said to me earlier this year: 'You know – I think that the sixties were more influenced by the fifties than they were by the seventies.' I agreed with him. Furthermore, the fifties were more influenced by the thirties and the forties than they were by the sixties which, you may remember, hadn't yet happened. In many ways, the first half of the fifties was still pre-war.

The chairman's question was certainly a pre-war question, but I thought I should nevertheless answer it truthfully. Until a month before I'd been absolutely broke but then I'd sold a one-hour drama script to BBC radio. In 1954, the BBC paid radio writers a guinea a minute – so a one-hour Wednesday matinee play earned £63. This practice of paying for length rather than quality had – as you might expect – a fundamental effect on playwriting technique. Whenever you wrote: *'There is a long pause'* you knew you'd earned half-a-crown. Even better: *'For some 30 seconds we hear nothing but the shrill call of seagulls'* was worth ten bob.

Quite long books have been written by scholars of the theatre trying to identify the cultural precedents that most influenced Harold Pinter. All they really needed to know was that in the 1950s long silences paid good money.

So I said to the chairman (who, you may remember, had asked me this question) '43 pounds'. Because that was how much I had left. He slapped his leather-topped desk in delight at my inventiveness and hired me immediately.

Well, very nearly immediately, anyway. It was such a gentlemanly place that they offered me a choice of remuneration: would I prefer £500 a year or £10 a week? In those days, annual pay was salary and went to gentlemen, and weekly pay was wages and went to – well, all the other people. Quick as always with the mental arithmetic, I went for the wages.

As it happens, 1954 was the last pre-war year because the next year, you may remember, was 1955 – and things were never the same again.

It was because of the imminence of commercial television that I had been hired in the first place. I'd written some undergraduate review material which had been produced first at Oxford, then on the Edinburgh fringe and later still in a small, underground club theatre in London. There were some songs and some humorous sketches. You may judge for yourself just how humorous the humorous sketches were because I shall now describe one to you.

In this particular humorous sketch, the object of my satirical attention was the then advertising campaign for Horlicks malted milk. You will remember that it took the form of stories told in strip continuity style. A person was failing in his job; he would go to the doctor who told him that there was nothing organically wrong with him, it was just that he was suffering from what we doctors call Night Starvation. The patient should drink a cup of hot Horlicks every night at bedtime starting forthwith. Quite soon afterwards, the hero became managing director and/or won a Nobel Peace Prize.

My first breakthrough was to realise just how very humorous it would be if a person whose job demanded that he remain awake at night should start to drink Horlicks and as a direct consequence get fired. My second breakthrough was to realise that the first breakthrough would have an even greater comic effect if the sketch were to be written in rhyming couplets. Oh, my. I was hot in those days.

So I made my hero a fireman, who said things like:

'Though I get all the sleep that is required
I always seem to wake up feeling tired.
I really cannot think why this should be
I think there must be something wrong with me.'

With his wife, he goes to see the doctor. The wife says:

'Though he gets all the sleep that is required
He always seems to wake up feeling tired.'

It's not widely known that these were among the first words uttered on the London stage by Maggie Smith. Within a few years, she was playing Desdemona opposite Olivier. It's extraordinary what good writing can do for otherwise quite workaday actors.

The revue was produced by Ned Sherrin and bits of it, including this richly comic sketch, were picked up by the BBC and turned into a 40-minute television programme – which must have reached an audience of well over several hundred people. One of these people, as it turned out, was the then head of the art department of J. Walter Thompson who was extremely anxious to outflank the then head of the copy department in gaining control of the vibrant new forthcoming medium. Since this revue had appeared on television, it seemed logical to the head of the art department that those of us who had written and produced it must know all about television. In fact, of course, we knew absolutely nothing about television. He was also much taken by the comic fireman sketch since J. Walter Thompson was the agency that had invented the Night Starvation campaign. So a letter went off inviting us to come in and have a chat, which both Ned and I duly did, and the unanimous view in 40 Berkeley Square was that Ned had little to offer the television medium whereas I did.

Four years later, I was the writer/producer on the Horlicks account. I'm a great admirer of the Almighty – I'd like Him to know that – but I particularly admire his sense of plot, shape and irony. Getting me to become the writer/producer on the Horlicks account must have given him quite a few private chuckles I should imagine.

In 1958, Horlicks was still a private, family company. The board was made up of the Horlick family itself, one or two hired managers of a lower social status altogether, and a number of delightful non-executive directors.

They were all getting on a bit and they were mostly Earls and Duchesses and Baronets and they all lived in places like Ross & Cromarty and Rutland. Their great treat came once a year when they set out for London in their Lagondas and sedan chairs to take up residence in, as I remember, this very hotel. Here they had an absolutely spiffing dinner and then met again the following morning to approve the year's advertising. And for something like 20 years, the advertising they'd been asked to approve had all been strip continuities about Night Starvation appearing in the newspapers, and they knew all about it and knew that it was good.

But 1958 was three years after 1955 and everything had changed. In 1958, for the very first time, Horlicks was going to be advertised on television – and it was to be my proud privilege to present the work.

A week beforehand, I met the managing director – a commoner, as I recall – and he gave me a very thorough briefing. The main point he made was that I would be unwise to assume that the members of the board would be at all familiar with the nature of the television medium itself. Some of them might well have heard of it, he told me, but none would have been actually exposed to it as such.

The day arrived and so did the board, seething and chuntering away with suppressed excitement. One of them, I remember, handed round a bag of humbugs.

I began. I explained that there had recently been a most interesting development in communications. It was, I said, a form of wireless set – but a wireless set combined with moving pictures not unlike a bioscope. It had come to be called 'television'. Many ordinary people, I explained – servants and that sort of person – now had television sets in their drawing rooms on which they would watch news programmes and musical comedies and other popular attractions. Furthermore, I told them, it was now possible to place advertisements on this television in much the same way as it had always been possible to place advertisements in newspapers, and, this year, that was precisely what their company proposed to do. There were going to be moving advertisements, with sound, for Horlicks, on television sets in millions of ordinary people's homes. They looked at each other in excited disbelief.

The commercials had already been made, and the agency had recently installed an extremely expensive closed-circuit system so that the films could be shown on television monitors. I pointed to these monitors, telling the board that these were not dissimilar to the kind of apparatus now to be found in ordinary people's homes – but that usually there was only one. I then phoned through to the boys in the back room and asked them to run the films.

In total silence, the films were shown. The silence held.

'Is that all?' said one peer. So, naturally, we showed them again.

And again there was silence.

'Just one thing,' said another. 'Just wonder, Chairman, if I might, through you ... wasn't absolutely certain what the policeman was doin'.' And the chairman nodded and looked to me for a comment.

Now I'd written and produced those commercials and I must have seen them 50 times. Even so, I had to check my memory to be absolutely sure. Not only was there no policeman in any of them but there wasn't even anyone who might remotely have been mistaken for a policeman. So I said, forced by desperation to resort to veracity: 'As a matter of fact, sir, there *wasn't* a policeman.'

And with absolutely no hesitation the peer said: 'In that case, I think they're absolutely first class.'

And so the half-million pound budget was enthusiastically approved – the equivalent of five million or more today. And they had a terrific lunch and home they went to Rutland.

That was in 1958, and it was probably the last pre-war advertising meeting ever to be held in this country.

The coming of commercial television remains by far the biggest single change to our trade over the whole of that 35 years.

It was at about this time that I was privileged to witness the birth of corporate advertising as we now know it. This story has never before been told in public.

The agency had recently been appointed by Cyril Lord. Cyril Lord, you will remember, sold carpets – and he claimed to sell them very cheaply because he'd cut out the middleman. There were no shops, you understand – Cyril Lord sold his carpets straight off the page. If the ad didn't generate sales, there *were* no sales.

J. Walter Thompson studied his previous campaign and concluded that it was very vulgar indeed. Instead of the eight-inch doubles – remember them? – we prepared an elegant and extremely expensive double-page spread for the *Sunday Express*. Just acres of carpet and a few bits of Chippendale to give it a homey look. At the very last minute, the art director was persuaded to include a small coupon.

The first ad ran – and after ten days, seven people had responded. We knew from an analysis of previous advertising that we could expect some 15 per cent of generated leads to be converted to sales. We could therefore confidently look forward, having used no more than 20 per cent of that year's total advertising budget, to making one sale.

Cyril Lord – in person – telephoned several times a day. It hardly helped at all when an eighth coupon arrived. The agency called a crisis meeting of very senior people to see what could be done – but there were few useful ideas.

Then one of our directors spoke. 'Just an idea,' he said, taking off his glasses and polishing them for emphasis. 'May be nothing in it, of course. But one thing we could do is take out the coupon altogether and call it a corporate ad.'

Nearly 30 years later, this test still works. Look at any corporate advertisement running today and ask yourself how many people would respond if it carried a coupon. If you can confidently say none, then it deserves the very highest praise and a D & AD gold pencil.

To nobody's surprise, Cyril Lord took his account away and gave it to a provincial upstart called Peter Marsh, who produced some extremely vulgar television advertising which sold many square miles of luxury carpet you can afford and made Mr Lord – for a little while at least – very rich. It also, rather later, made Mr Marsh very poor indeed – but luckily that didn't last long either.

It was exactly this kind of advertising – or to be fair, television advertising in general – that began to have an extremely adverse effect on the reputation of advertising as a trade – at any rate among the chattering classes.

Television advertising possessed two characteristics which the middle classes found intolerable. First, it was intrusive – which is to say that it was noticed. And second, it worked. Here was clear evidence that vulnerable and unsophisticated people – in other words, the sort of people who would watch television – were being manipulated, almost certainly subliminally, by sociology graduates who had been brainwashed by capitalism. It wasn't, of course, necessary to have read *The Hidden Persuaders* to know precisely what was going on. As long as all advertising had remained as inoffensive and invisible as corporate advertising, we'd never have had any of that trouble – but trouble we got all right and it was all television's fault. Before the explosion came, the fuse burned slowly for nearly 20 years – but I'm getting ahead of myself again.

1969 is memorable for having been the year in which the least memorable advertising event of the last 35 years took place.

For months and months, agencies and production companies gave presentations, conference companies laid on conferences, advertisers sent delegates on expensive training courses and the trade papers did their best to sustain a ferment of speculation. It was the biggest thing to happen to commercial television since commercial television, and you've all forgotten. It was of course colour.

When I was asked for the tenth time by the trade press how quickly colour television was going to take off, I said I thought the official industry forecast was probably right, but of course if it so happened that the Queen was assassinated and the country was given nine months to prepare for the coronation of King Charles, then the penetration of colour television sets might well take place with somewhat greater speed. Two weeks later the *New Statesman* ran a small piece in This England: 'How to boost colour TV sales? Adman Jeremy Bullimore advocates killing Queen.'

Like most of my recommendations, this was ignored. Colour came and stayed and nobody's mentioned it for 20 years until this evening and that will certainly do for another 20 years.

Meanwhile the fuse was still burning and the bang nearly happened in 1974.

1974, you may remember, was not a good year for Ted Heath.

Come to think of it, he hasn't had many good years since. He lost two elections, and at the Advertising Association conference that year Shirley Williams and the first Director

General of Fair Trading, John Methven, told us what they thought of the advertising business and its voluntary controls.

Threats of statutory controls of a quite unworkable kind were really not very far away. At that same conference, Ronnie Kirkwood and I attempted to put another point of view – which was more or less encapsulated in a short duologue. It went like this:

Good morning.

Good morning? Good in relation to what? Do you mean in the sense of having desirable qualities?

I mean hullo.

Then why didn't you say so? I might have been misled.

But you weren't.

I wasn't misled – but many people less perceptive and less well-educated than I might have been misled.

Don't you think that everyone knows that 'good morning' is simply a greeting?

Are you saying that the word good has become so debased by people like you that it no longer carries its true meaning?

The phrase has been around for a long time.

So have prostitution, poverty, corruption, white slavery and child-beating. Are you saying that anything's defensible if it's been around long enough?

Almost everyone says 'good morning'.

And almost everyone exceeds the speed limit.

I can't help feeling this conversation is getting out of proportion.

Are you suggesting that deliberate attempts to mislead, the debasement of language, white slavery, child-beating and the mowing down at speed of defenceless pedestrians are matters of minor concern?

No – I was suggesting that saying 'good morning' wasn't quite the same as white slavery.

And white slavery isn't the same as child-beating, I suppose. Can't you appreciate that *degree* is no defence?

I don't think saying 'good morning' is anything to be ashamed of.

Which is precisely what concerns me. You say 'good morning', admit that you didn't mean to suggest that the morning was good, become defensive in the extreme, retreat behind endless excuses of precedent and common practice and then say you've nothing to be ashamed of.

Most people become defensive when they're attacked.

But why? Why can't they admit the attack is justified and mend their ways?

All right then. I concede. Goodbye.

Why are you saying 'goodbye'?

Because I'm going away now.

Are you suggesting that your going will have certain desirable qualities ?

Yes.

Debates about advertising control had sunk to about that level. The risk of statutory control was real and imminent. To its immense and lasting credit, the trade acted very quickly and very well. The Advertising Standards Board of Finance was formed (ASBOF, now of course more widely known as the acronym for the Amalgamated Society of Boring Old Farts), the levy was invented and the Advertising Standards Authority was strengthened – and a great many people these days don't even know what happened and how lucky they still are.

Four years later, Roy Hattersley – as he then was – told a conference in Bournemouth that he was opposed to excessive statutory control. It was interesting to learn that Mr Hattersley was opposed to excess, but it didn't win many votes and the subject went quiet. It will not, however, remain quiet for all time.

Meanwhile, the advertising trade was suffering from an acute loss of self-confidence. The agency business has always been pretty insecure, of course. Take 1927, for example – (you thought I was making progress, didn't you?) only a deeply insecure bunch of people would choose to call themselves, as far back as 1927, The Institute of Practitioners in Advertising.

They were of course what they are now – advertisement agents; but desperately searching for respectability. That's why they invented exams for themselves. I expect some of you even took the IPA exams. There was one question – a real one – which asked candidates to draw up a marketing plan for a new range of knee-high fashion boots for men. I often wondered who scored well on that one.

Imprudently – and impertinently – I suggested that the questions were nothing to do with how to be a good agency person: they were all to do with irrelevant matters such as knowledge and experience. So I made so bold as to draft some better questions which I put to the IPA, and I can still remember three of them:

1. You are an account executive. You arrive late for a meeting in Carlisle, at which you are to show your client next year's television planning for a range of aerosol pudding-tops. On opening your chart-case, you discover that you've brought with you three press layouts for earth-moving equipment. In five minutes, relevantly, relate the latter to the former.

2. You are the chairman of a middle-sized agency. You read in *Campaign* that your managing director and three of your other directors have resigned, taking with them your one profitable account and both your top creative men. Draft a letter to your remaining clients explaining how these changes will dramatically improve the quality of your service.

3. One of your older clients has just appointed a new marketing director fresh from Procter & Gamble. In the course of your first meeting, he turns to you and says: 'But

surely you have to agree that the frequency distribution of dosage-weighted opportunities to see can only be related to average issue readership of press media by application of response functions derived from single-source data?' By means of a diagram or a rough sketch, illustrate the most responsible facial expression with which this remark should be greeted.

I argued that those were *real* questions, designed to identify real talent for the real agency world. The IPA disagreed – and not long afterwards abandoned examinations altogether. And not long after that, the reputation of advertising again began to burgeon.

From 1979 onwards, advertising became a thoroughly good thing *for* anything, *in* anything, however much – and the government joined in enthusiastically. Junior ministers in the Thatcher administration began to ask for Tim Bell's autograph. Lord Young should certainly have received the Mackintosh Medal for services to advertising.

These days, of course, I rely on the newspapers and very old friends to keep me in touch with the challenging, dynamic, fast-moving world I still fondly if dimly remember. I was therefore grateful to the *Observer Magazine* of some 12 days ago for bringing me absolutely up to date in time for this important engagement with you this evening.

The creative director of a London agency is quoted. He says: 'I wear a suit once a week. I adjust what I wear depending on which clients I'm meeting. The myth of advertising has been blown out of all proportion. Basically, to succeed one has to be professional, have charisma and be able to produce a great commercial for half the price that another agency could.' That is all he says.

I'm afraid I didn't know any of that. How easy it is to get out of touch.

Bibliography

Bernstein, D. *Creative Advertising: For This You Went To Oxford* (1976)

de Bono, E. *The Use of Lateral Thinking* (1966)

Dunkley, C. *Television Today and Tomorrow*, Harmondsworth, Penguin Books (1985)

Fletcher, W. *Teach Yourself Advertising*, Hodder & Stoughton (1978)

Galton, F. *Statistical Inquiries into the Efficacy of Prayer*, Fortnightly Review (1872)

Gardner, B.B. & Levy, S.J. 'The product and the brand', *Harvard Business Review*, March/April (1955)

Hopkins, C. *My Life in Advertising/Scientific Advertising*, Advertising Publications Inc (1966)

King, S. *Developing New Brands*, Pitman (1973), JWT (1984)

Koestler, A. *The Act of Creation*, Hutchinson (1964), Penguin (1975)

Magee, B. *Popper*, Fontana Modern Masters (1985)

Medawar, P.B *Induction and Intuition in Scientific Thought*, Methuen (University Paperbacks) (1969)

Medawar, P.B. *The Art of the Soluble*, Methuen (1967), Pelican Books (1969)

Medawar, P.B. *Pluto's Republic*, Oxford University Press (1982)

Medawar, P.B. Review of The Act of Creation, New Statesman, (July 1964)

Ogilvy, D. *Confessions of an Advertising Man*, Atheneum (1962)

Ogilvy, D. *Ogilvy on Advertising*, Crown Publishers Inc (1983)

Packard, V. *The Hidden Persuaders* (1957)

Peters, T. & Waterman, R. *In Search of Excellence*, Harper &
    Row (1982)
Reeves, R. *Reality in Advertising*, Alfred Knopf (1961)
Young, J.W. *How to Become an Advertising Man*, Advertising
    Publications Inc (1963)
Young, J.W. *A Technique for Producing Ideas,* Crain Books
    (1975), NTC Business Book (1989)
Williamson, J. *Decoding Advertisements: Idealogy and
    Meaning in Advertising*, Open Forum, Marion Boyers
    (1978)